101 THINGS YOU DIDN'T KNOW ABOUT

WORLD WAR I

The People, Battles, and *Aftermath of the Great War*

ERIK SASS

Author of *The Mental Floss History of the United States*

D1532420

ADAMS MEDIA

NEW YORK LONDON TORONTO SYDNEY NEW DELHI

Adams Media
An Imprint of Simon & Schuster, Inc.
57 Littlefield Street
Avon, Massachusetts 02322

First Adams Media trade paperback edition September 2018

ADAMS MEDIA and colophon are trademarks of Simon & Schuster.

For information about special discounts for bulk purchases, please contact Simon & Schuster Special Sales at 1-866-506-1949 or business@simonandschuster.com.

The Simon & Schuster Speakers Bureau can bring authors to your live event. For more information or to book an event contact the Simon & Schuster Speakers Bureau at 1-866-248-3049 or visit our website at www.simonspeakers.com.

Interior images by Eric Andrews

Manufactured in the United States of America

10 9 8 7 6 5 4 3 2

Library of Congress Cataloging-in-Publication Data
Sass, Erik, author.
101 things you didn't know about World War I / Erik Sass, author of The Mental Floss History of the United States.
Avon, Massachusetts: Adams Media, 2018.
Series: 101 things.
Includes index.
LCCN 2018011465 | ISBN 9781507207222 (pb) | ISBN 9781507207239 (ebook)
Subjects: LCSH: World War, 1914-1918. | World War, 1914-1918--Campaigns.
Classification: LCC D521 .S335 2018 | DDC 940.3--dc23
LC record available at https://lccn.loc.gov/2018011465

ISBN 978-1-5072-0722-2
ISBN 978-1-5072-0723-9 (ebook)

CONTENTS

Contents

Contents

Contents

Contents

Contents

INTRODUCTION

From 1914–1918, Europe's Great Powers, supposedly representing the height of human progress, tore themselves to pieces with all the destructive power of modern weaponry. They left 12 million soldiers and 8 million civilians dead, plus millions more mutilated or disabled. The war swept away old ways of life, introducing a strange modern world of mechanization and mass culture. At home, "total war" meant total mobilization of society; millions of women and children marched off to work as men marched off to the trenches.

In many ways we're still living in the shadow of the First World War. That's why it's so important that we understand what happened and why.

101 Things You Didn't Know about World War I explores that question: What happened? How could ordinary people suddenly lapse into an orgy of hate-fueled killing? Along the way we'll discover the personalities who directed the war on both sides as well as learn about the people who fought and died in it.

Before we begin, though, we need to know how the stage was set for this great conflict.

Historical Background

While it's impossible to reduce such a complex event as World War I to a single cause, one thing stands out: nationalism. Starting in the fifteenth century nationalism became a motivating force in people's lives. People needed a shared identity and story. Nationalism, a new emotional force, drew on shared language, ethnicity, legends, and achievements to reassure people they were still part of something bigger than themselves. The nation would endure, remember them, and take care of their children after they were gone; in return, they'd embrace and fight for their country.

Nationalism spread across Europe and later the world, often encouraged by rulers looking for ways to unite and motivate their subjects. However, it could also disrupt things: after the French Revolution, French nationalism under Napoleon Bonaparte overturned the European order, and later Europe's delicate balance of power was upset by the formation of two new nation-states, Germany and Italy.

Germany's fast-growing population and industrial power intimidated Britain and France, who were nervous about its plans to build a great navy and compete with them for colonies; the French also resented the loss of Alsace-Lorraine, provinces on the border of France annexed by Germany in 1871. Their fears prompted France to form an alliance with Russia and cooperate with Britain. The Germans felt they were being "encircled."

At the same time a new wave of nationalism in Eastern Europe and the Balkans threatened the old empires there: Austria-Hungary, Russia, and the Ottoman Empire. Ethnic groups trapped in the old medieval realms wanted out. The Ottoman Empire in particular was on its last legs, as various peoples in the Balkans threw off the Turkish yoke and established new nations.

But Balkan borders were far from stable: in the First and Second Balkan Wars, 1912–1913, the new nations fought first the Ottoman Empire and then each other for its remaining European territories. Even worse, Austria-Hungary (which already faced internal nationalist movements) waded deeper into this explosive situation by annexing Bosnia-Herzegovina, an old Ottoman province, in 1908.

Many Bosnian Serbs would rather have joined the neighboring Slavic kingdom of Serbia. Austria-Hungary was determined to destroy Serbian nationalism before it tore the empire apart. But there was one big problem: Serbia was backed up by Russia, traditional patron of the Slavic kingdoms in the Balkan Peninsula.

Between Germany's fear of encirclement and its ally Austria-Hungary's fear of rising nationalism, by 1914 Europe was ready to explode. All it needed was someone to light a match.

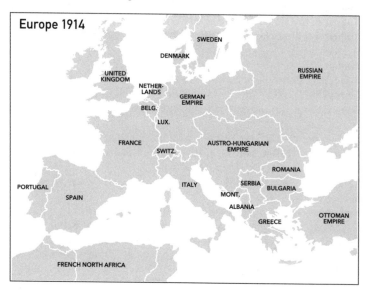

Timeline of the First World War

1914

- **June 28:** Bosnian Serb nationalist Gavrilo Princip assassinates Archduke Franz Ferdinand, heir to the throne of Austria-Hungary, in Sarajevo
- **July 5:** Austro-Hungarian diplomat Count Alexander von Hoyos visits Berlin, receives "blank check"—a promise Germany will back Austria-Hungary no matter what
- **July 23:** Austria-Hungary delivers an ultimatum to Serbia containing demands certain to be rejected, providing an excuse for war
- **July 24–27:** European diplomats try to defuse mounting tension without success
- **July 28:** Austria-Hungary declares war on Serbia

- **July 29:** Last-ditch compromise, British proposal for a "Halt in Belgrade," rejected by Austria-Hungary
- **July 30:** Russia mobilizes against Austria-Hungary and Germany
- **August 1:** Germany declares war on Russia
- **August 3:** Germany declares war on France, invades neutral Belgium
- **August 4:** Britain declares war on Germany, imposes naval blockade
- **August 14:** French invade Germany but are repulsed in Battle of the Frontiers
- **August 17:** Two Russian armies invade East Prussia
- **August 20:** Germans occupy Brussels
- **August 30:** Russian Second Army is destroyed at Battle of Tannenberg
- **September 6–10:** German invasion of France fails at the "Miracle on the Marne"
- **September 11–13:** Germans dig in at Aisne, beginning trench warfare
- **September 17–October 19:** German and Allied armies try to outflank each other unsuccessfully in "Race to the Sea"
- **October 19:** Germans fail to break through Allied defenses at First Battle of Ypres
- **November 2:** Russia declares war on Ottoman Empire
- **November 16:** Serbs defeat Austro-Hungarian invasion at Battle of Kolubara
- **December 20:** French suffer huge losses in First Battle of Champagne
- **December 24–25:** German and British soldiers fraternize in Christmas Eve Truce

1915

- **February 4:** Germany declares unrestricted U-boat warfare around British Isles
- **March 10–13:** British score victory at Battle of Neuve Chapelle but fail to exploit success
- **April 22:** Germans use chlorine in first big gas attack at the Second Battle of Ypres
- **April 24:** Ottoman Turks unleash Armenian Genocide, killing 1.5 million by 1917
- **April 25:** Allied amphibious landings at Gallipoli fail to crack Turkish defenses
- **May 7:** German U-boat sinks *Lusitania*, killing 1,198 and outraging American opinion
- **May 23:** Italy declares war on Austria-Hungary, joins Allies
- **May 31:** First German zeppelin bombing raid against London
- **June 13:** Central Powers pierce Russian defenses at Gorlice-Tarnow, Russian "Great Retreat" begins, leading to German conquest of Poland and Lithuania

Retreat of the Russian army 1915

- **August 6:** Second Allied landing at Gallipoli fails at Suvla Bay
- **August 12:** Tsar Nicholas II takes personal command of Russian Army
- **August 26:** Germany bows to US demands, ends unrestricted U-boat warfare
- **September 21:** French mount new attack in Champagne, but it fails by October 15
- **September 25:** British launch huge attack at Loos, suffer bloody defeat
- **October 5:** Allies occupy Salonika, Greece in belated attempt to help Serbia
- **October 6:** Bulgaria joins Central Powers, helps crush Serbia by December
- **November 23:** Battered Serbian Army begins retreat through Albania
- **December 7:** Anglo-Indian forces in Mesopotamia (Iraq) besieged by Turks at Kut
- **December 19:** Allies evacuate Gallipoli, campaign ends in total failure

1916

- **January 27:** Britain adopts conscription, ending tradition of voluntary service
- **February 21–28:** Germans unleash biggest attack of the war yet at Verdun, but are halted by French
- **March 1:** Germans resume unrestricted U-boat warfare over American protests
- **March 24:** Sinking of passenger liner *Sussex* leads to new US-German conflict
- **April 15:** Allied ships transport Serbian survivors from Albania to island of Corfu
- **April 24–29:** Irish Easter Rising in Dublin crushed by British
- **April 29:** 15,000 Anglo-Indian troops surrender to Turks at Kut, Mesopotamia
- **May 8:** Germans back down on U-boat warfare a second time due to US threats
- **May 9:** British and French agree to divide up Middle East in Sykes-Picot agreement
- **May 31:** British and German fleets clash at Battle of Jutland, but outcome is indecisive
- **June 4:** Russians begin Brusilov Offensive, their most successful attack of the war
- **June 5:** Arabs under Grand Sharif Hussein and Prince Faisal revolt against Turks
- **July 1:** British suffer 50,000 casualties on first day of Battle of the Somme
- **July 23:** Russian Foreign Minister Sazonov fired, showing growing power of Rasputin
- **August 17:** Romania declares war on Austria-Hungary, joining Allies
- **August 29:** Hindenburg replaces Falkenhayn as top German commander, halts Verdun
- **September 3:** First zeppelin shot down by British plane with incendiary ammunition
- **September 15:** British use tanks for the first time at the Somme, with mixed success
- **September 27:** Central Powers unleash crushing counterattack against Romania
- **October 25:** T.E. Lawrence, a.k.a. "Lawrence of Arabia," meets Prince Faisal
- **November 7:** Woodrow Wilson wins reelection on slogan, "He Kept Us Out of War"
- **November 19:** Battle of the Somme ends in Allied failure

- **November 21:** Emperor Franz-Josef dies, Karl I takes throne of Austria-Hungary
- **November 27:** German long-distance bombers make first raid on Britain
- **December 7:** Central Powers capture Romanian capital, Bucharest
- **December 30:** Rasputin murdered by Russian courtiers

1917

- **January 11:** Germans start "Hindenburg Line," new defensive position in France
- **January 17:** British code-breakers intercept "Zimmermann Telegram" from Germany, urging Mexico to declare war on US
- **February 1–3:** Germany resumes unrestricted U-boat warfare; Wilson breaks off relations, but does not declare war
- **February 25:** British present evidence of Zimmermann Telegram to Wilson
- **March 8:** Protests on International Women's Day spark Russian Revolution in Petrograd
- **March 11:** British capture Baghdad after a new offensive in Mesopotamia
- **March 15:** Tsar Nicholas II abdicates; power is split between liberal Provisional Government and socialist Petrograd Soviet
- **April 6:** US declares war on Germany
- **April 16:** French "Nivelle Offensive" fails spectacularly on the Western Front
- **May 8:** French Army is crippled by a wave of mutinies, lasting until June
- **May 18:** Wilson signs US draft law, General John "Black Jack" Pershing named commander of the American Expeditionary Force
- **June 7:** British set off gigantic mine explosion to begin Battle of Messines
- **July 1:** Russian Provisional Government launches "Kerensky Offensive," last major campaign of the war, which ends in immediate failure
- **July 6:** Arab forces led by T.E. Lawrence capture Aqaba, key port on Red Sea
- **July 31:** British launch massive new offensive at Third Battle of Ypres (Passchendaele), but fail to break through German defenses by November
- **September 5–9:** Germans capture Riga, spurring fears of advance on Petrograd; conservative general Kornilov tries to overthrow Russia's Provisional Government but is defeated
- **October 12:** US "Rainbow Division" embarks for Europe
- **October 24:** Central Powers score huge victory at Caporetto, occupy northern Italy
- **October 30:** British gain foothold in Palestine at the Third Battle of Gaza
- **November 6:** Bolsheviks overthrow Provisional Government in second coup attempt

- **November 8:** Balfour Declaration states British support for Jewish homeland
- **November 20:** British launch surprise attack with tanks at Cambrai, but Germans soon recapture lost ground
- **December 11:** Anglo-Egyptian forces capture Jerusalem
- **December 17:** Bolsheviks, Central Powers agree on armistice at Brest-Litovsk

1918

- **January 8:** Wilson presents "Fourteen Points," idealistic plan for post-war world
- **January 20:** Central Powers sign peace agreement with Ukraine
- **February 6:** British Parliament grants women aged 30+ right to vote
- **March 3:** Bolsheviks sign Treaty of Brest-Litovsk, allowing Germans to shift troops to the Western Front for a new offensive
- **March 21–28:** Germans unleash giant attack, "Operation Michael," on the Western Front in bid to defeat Britain and France before American troops arrive in Europe in large numbers; offensive stalls despite the destruction of British Fifth Army
- **April 3:** Allies agree Ferdinand Foch will be new commander in chief of all forces

The Western Front in 1918

HOLLAND

BRUSSELS

BELGIUM

FRANCE

PARIS

Starting point for the Allied offensives, 8 August 1918.

- **April 9:** Germans launch second major offensive, "Operation Georgette"
- **April 21:** Max von Richthofen, "The Red Baron," dies when his plane is shot down
- **May 7:** Romania capitulates to Central Powers, Germany controls Ukraine
- **May 14:** Czech Legion, made up of freed POWs in Russia, revolts against Bolsheviks
- **May 22:** Spanish press, free from war censorship, reports influenza epidemic; it will go on to kill approximately 50–100 million people around the world—more than the war
- **May 27:** Germans launch third major offensive, "Operation Blücher-Yorck," on the Aisne, but it stalls within a week
- **June 2:** Pershing agrees to transport 250,000 US troops per month to Europe
- **June 9–14:** Fourth German offensive, "Operation Gneisenau," fails thanks to US troops
- **July 1:** Food shortage reaching crisis proportions in Central Powers
- **July 15–19:** Last major German offensive of the war on Western Front, *Kaiserschlact*, or Kaiser's Battle, fails; Foch orders major counterattack; Bolsheviks execute Romanovs
- **July 26:** American and French troops advance 10 miles in the Marne sector
- **August 8:** "Black Day of the Germany Army," German forces are in retreat along entire Western Front
- **August 10:** US First Army formed for attack on St. Mihiel salient; over 1.4 million US troops in France
- **August 23:** Allies launch new offensive along entire front from Soissons to Arras
- **September 5:** Bolsheviks unleash "Red Terror" in Russia, killing thousands
- **September 10:** Hindenburg tells the kaiser they must end the war at once
- **September 23:** Anti-Bolshevik "White" forces form "All-Russian Government" in Siberia
- **September 24:** Allies advance into southern Serbia, Bulgarians ask for armistice
- **October 1:** Arab Army, Australian cavalry capture Damascus
- **October 4–5:** Central Powers send notes to Wilson asking for peace negotiations
- **October 14:** Wilson demands end of U-boat warfare for peace
- **October 18:** Wilson demands Austria-Hungary free nationalities; Turks request armistice
- **October 23:** Wilson demands Germany create constitutional government for peace

- **October 28:** German sailors mutiny, launching German Revolution
- **October 30:** Turks accept Allied armistice demands, Austria recognizes Czechoslovakia
- **October 31:** Hungarians proclaim independent republic, end of monarchy
- **November 1:** Austrian socialists proclaim republic, end of empire; French free Belgrade
- **November 4:** Austrians, Hungarians accept Allied armistice terms
- **November 9:** Kaiser Wilhelm II abdicates, flees Germany for Netherlands
- **November 11:** German, Allied representatives sign armistice agreement

PART 1

The Coming of War

THE FIRST WORLD War is often described as the "war nobody wanted," and it's true none of the participants wanted the war the way it turned out. But all of Europe's Great Powers had their own long-term goals, and some of these were in direct conflict.

Austria-Hungary's multiethnic realm was rocked by the rise of nationalism. Slavs, Italians, and Romanians demanded self-determination or—even worse—unification with ethnic kinsmen in neighboring countries. The worst trouble spot was the Balkans, where Austria-Hungary's foolish decision to annex Bosnia, a province of the decaying Ottoman Empire, put it on a collision course with the neighboring Kingdom of Serbia in 1908. Backed by their Slavic patron, Russia, the Serbs encouraged pan-Serbian and Yugoslav nationalist movements in Austria-Hungary. Fearing Slavic nationalism as an existential threat to the multinational empire, Austria-Hungary's leaders were determined to crush Serbia once and for all.

As well, the "Triple Entente" of France, Russia, and Britain (later the Allies) did their part to set the stage for war. French nationalists wanted to "redeem" Alsace-Lorraine, annexed by the German Empire after

France's defeat by Prussia in 1871. The Russians were backing Serbian nationalists to stir up trouble in Austria-Hungary because they wanted to grab Austrian Galicia for themselves; they were also plotting to seize the ailing Ottoman Empire's capital, Constantinople (now Istanbul), and the strategic Turkish straits, which could choke off Russia's maritime trade routes via the Black Sea. For its part Britain stood aside as always—but its informal partnership with France and Russia encouraged them to take a more aggressive stance toward Germany and Austria-Hungary.

By the beginning of 1914 the Slavic nationalist threat looked more menacing than ever. Austria-Hungary's chief of the general staff, Conrad von Hötzendorf, had a simple solution: war with Serbia.

Not everyone supported the plan: the heir to the throne, Archduke Franz Ferdinand, was much more conciliatory to the Serbs. But Franz Ferdinand was still waiting in the wings, while Hötzendorf exercised growing influence over Foreign Minister Count Leopold von Berchtold and Emperor Franz Josef, who were also being urged to settle the Serbian business by their powerful German ally. All they needed was an excuse to attack Serbia.

1

One More Alliance Might Have Helped

Safe on their islands, protected by the world's biggest navy, the British had long enjoyed "splendid isolation" from the rest of Europe, only fighting when they felt their interests were at stake. By the early twentieth century, however, the rise of Germany forced Britain to form closer relationships with other European powers, especially its age-old foe, France. Alarmed by Germany's growing power, Britain and France worked out their colonial differences in a "friendly understanding" in order to present a united front in Europe...sort of.

The British suffered from extreme commitment phobia. Conservative to the end, Prime Minister Herbert Asquith and Foreign Secretary Edward Grey couldn't bring themselves to give up Britain's traditional independence by signing a formal alliance. Still, the German threat was clear, and more pragmatic voices warned that in the event of all-out war, there was no way Britain could stand aside.

In the absence of a formal alliance, a few senior cabinet members including Asquith and Grey secretly gave the soldiers permission to begin working with their French counterparts behind the scenes, informally—just in case. British and French officers hammered out the details for military cooperation, while Britain technically remained free of any obligation to help France.

> "The fact is, all of Europe is on a hair trigger, and all are ready except England, who seems as careless and reckless as she is ignorant."
> —*General Henry Wilson, November 1912*

The closest Britain and France ever came to an alliance was a "naval convention," signed in 1912, which gave France responsibility for patrolling the Mediterranean so Britain could concentrate its battleships on the German threat in the North Sea. They also secretly agreed, during future crises, to "immediately discuss with the other, whether both Governments should act together to prevent aggression and to preserve peace"—not exactly an ironclad promise by Britain to do, well, anything. As late as April 1914, Grey could affirm to Parliament that Britain still enjoyed "freedom from all obligations to engage in military operations on the Continent."

In the end, British ambiguity probably helped bring about war, by encouraging the French and their Russian allies to take a more aggressive stance toward Germany, while failing to convince the Germans that the British really meant business—in short, the "worst of both worlds."

2

Battleships by Subscription

From 1910–1913 Europe was gripped by an arms race as the "Great Powers" splashed out huge sums on ever-bigger armies and navies. Driven by Germany's fear of "encirclement"—ironically brought on by its own bellicose behavior—the Teutonic spending spree provoked countering moves by Britain, France, and Russia. Meanwhile Austria-Hungary faced off with Italy, and the Ottoman Empire was shaken awake by its defeat at the hands of Serbia, Bulgaria, and Greece in the First Balkan War in 1912.

Still, ultrapatriotic types on all sides protested that their countries were losing the arms race, vilifying opponents as naïve or worse—traitors.

"The Admiralty had demanded six ships; the economists offered four; and we finally compromised on eight."
—*Winston Churchill*

These sorts of sentiments weren't limited to Britain and Germany. In fact, the soaring cost of naval armaments prompted militarists in the Ottoman Empire to embrace a unique means of funding new construction: popular subscriptions, appealing to patriotic sentiment to raise money for enormous battleships otherwise beyond the national budget.

After taking power in a revolution in 1908, the "Young Turks" of the Committee of Union and Progress (CUP) placed a flurry of orders for new battleships with foreign (mainly British) shipyards. However, their nemesis Russia cut off most sources of international finance through diplomatic means. To fill the gap the CUP founded a quasi-official propaganda and marketing organization, the Ottoman Navy Foundation, which whipped up patriotic fervor among the Turkish middle classes by highlighting foreign threats and hearkening back to naval glories of bygone days.

The centerpiece of the new fleet purchased by the Ottoman Navy Foundation was an intimidating super-dreadnought battleship ordered in 1911, the *Reşadiye*—560 feet long with a top speed of 31 knots, armed with ten 13.5-inch guns, each capable of throwing a 1,400-pound shell over 13 miles. After the disastrous First Balkan War in 1912, the Navy Foundation bought another super-dreadnought, the *Sultan Osman I*, from the British shipyards of Vickers-Armstrong. Both dreadnoughts would play a critical role in the Ottoman Empire's entry into the First World War—even though neither ever joined the Turkish Navy.

Immediately following Britain's declaration of war on Germany on August 4, 1914, First Lord of the Admiralty Winston Churchill requisitioned both battleships for the Royal Navy, under the names *Erin* and *Agincourt*. Although the British promised compensation, Turkish public opinion was outraged, and Germany, desperately seeking more allies, saw an opportunity.

Two powerful German warships, the battle cruiser *Goeben* and the light cruiser *Breslau*, were on patrol in the Mediterranean Sea when war broke out. Dodging British fleets, from July 28 to August 10, 1914 the ships made a successful dash for the Ottoman capital Constantinople, where the Turks purchased them for a nominal sum. The replacement of their lost warships salved wounded Turkish pride, swinging public opinion firmly in Germany's court.

German sailors donned Turkish uniforms, and the *Goeben* and *Breslau*, renamed the *Yavuz Sultan Selim* and *Midili*, soon played a decisive role bringing the Ottoman Empire into the war. When the Ottoman cabinet dragged its feet declaring war, in November 1914 the German admiralty ordered the "Turkish" ships to mount a surprise attack on Russian ships and ports in the Black Sea, settling the issue. Now the Turkish government had no choice but to throw in their lot with Germany, sealing the fate of the Ottoman Empire.

Did the Schlieffen Plan Exist?

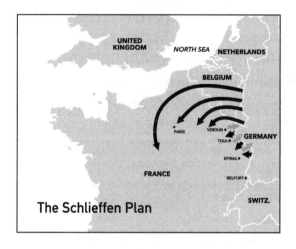

The Schlieffen Plan

According to conventional wisdom, by the time of his retirement in 1906, German chief of the general staff Alfred von Schlieffen had perfected an invincible plan to annihilate the French Army through a giant battle of encirclement, requiring a lunge through Belgium made possible by using reserve divisions in the front lines. The strategy called for a strong right wing to punch through Belgium and northern France, encircling Paris from the west, while the weak left wing went on the defensive, possibly even luring some French armies to attack them; after swiftly defeating France, victorious German troops would immediately be sent east to defeat France's ally Russia. Of course, the proposed violation of Belgian neutrality risked provoking Britain to declare war on Germany.

Critics of German militarism have long pointed to the plan as proof that Germany actively planned a war of conquest in the west, while some of Schlieffen's peers dismissed it as too mechanical. Among other constraints, Germany had to defeat France in about six weeks, before Russia could complete its lengthy mobilization. That meant that as soon as Russia started mobilizing, the clock was ticking for Germany to invade and conquer France—the Germans had no choice but to attack.

It's not quite that simple: in fact, Schlieffen himself had dismissed the plan as impracticable. By his own admission in his final memorandum on the subject in 1905, even with the use of reserve divisions the plan still had a shortfall of up to eight army corps or 200,000 men—enough for two more armies—needed to extend the German right wing around Paris. The troops didn't exist, and even if they did, it would require a feat of logistics to wedge them in alongside the others. Schlieffen predicted:

Make these preparations how we may, we shall reach the conclusion that we are too weak to continue operations in this direction. We shall find the experience of all earlier conquerors confirmed, that a war of aggression calls for much strength and also consumes much, that this strength dwindles constantly as the defender's increases, and all this particularly so in a country which bristles with fortresses.

In short, Schlieffen didn't recommend a bold attack on France through Belgium at all. Instead, based on previously unpublished manuscripts, the revisionist historian Terence Zuber argues that Schlieffen actually favored a much more modest swing through Belgium to attack the French fortress line—Verdun, Toul, Épinal, and Belfort—from both directions. Germany could then use its rail mobility and the advantage of interior lines to send troops east to defend East Prussia against looming Russian invasion.

Schlieffen didn't envision a knockout blow on either front. Instead he looked for defensive victories against a numerically superior foe, with more campaigns or perhaps a negotiated peace to follow. The need to make troops available to defend East Prussia became even more pressing in the years 1910–1913, as the Russian Army completed its recovery from its disastrous defeat by Japan in 1905. Russia's construction of new military railroads and implementation of hidden "pre-mobilization" measures, speeding up mobilization significantly, also made the alleged six-week timeframe for defeating France look more and more unlikely.

According to Zuber, Schlieffen's successor, Helmuth von Moltke "the Younger," actually tried to implement this alternative war plan, threatening the French frontier fortress line from the rear via Belgium and northern France. But even this more limited campaign failed when the German First Army turned to face the new French Sixth Army north of Paris, preventing it from protecting the flank of the German Second Army.

Zuber argues the "Schlieffen Plan" was invented after the war by the general staff archives as a way to pin blame for their failure during the invasion of France on the hapless Moltke, a conveniently deceased scapegoat. By creating a legend that Schlieffen handed down a perfect plan to defeat France, but that Moltke failed to understand it, they maintained the legend of the invincibility of the German general staff while distracting attention from their own mistakes.

4

Trench Warfare Was Predicted

Trench warfare confounded commanders on all sides, who seemed unable to grasp tactical developments that gave defenders a decisive advantage over attackers, no matter how brave. But it was hardly the unforeseeable tragedy generals later claimed (often to excuse their own shortcomings). In fact, trench warfare had been predicted in detail decades before.

Jan Gotlib Bloch (1836–1902) was a Polish Jewish banker with no military service or particular expertise in military affairs but a keen intelligence and the resources to devote to the study of technical developments in weaponry. In his professional life Bloch also participated in the construction of Russia's railroad network, giving him a window into this important aspect of modern military planning.

Following the Franco-Prussian War of 1870–1871, fascinated by rapid changes in military technology, Bloch began analyzing current doctrine in light of new weapons and capabilities, including machine guns, fast-repeating rifles, smokeless gunpowder, and barbed wire, all produced on an industrial scale.

In a 3,084-page-long book, titled *Is War Now Impossible?*, Bloch argued that these developments had rendered current ideas about battlefield combat, centering on massed bayonet charges and cavalry maneuvers, totally obsolete. Defenders equipped with modern weapons would enjoy a four-to-one tactical advantage over attackers advancing over open terrain, simply mowing them down. Bloch further predicted this would force combatants to resort to entrenchment to shelter soldiers from enemy fire.

Because Bloch died in 1902—before the Wright Brothers' first flight and Henry Ford's development of automobile mass production—he couldn't foresee the contribution of tanks or airplanes. But his book was hailed as a triumph of technical analysis and an important argument against the European arms race. Bloch also addressed a personal appeal to the British people in a popular magazine. But the fact that he was an amateur gave Europe's military elites an excuse to brush aside his arguments (even after they were confirmed by events including the Boer War from 1899–1902 and the Russo-Japanese War in 1904–1905).

Barbed Wire

Barbed wire, invented by Lucian Smith of Kent, Ohio, in 1867, allowed American ranchers to easily enclose large areas of Western pastureland in places where wood for fences was scarce. In 1874 a rival inventor, Joseph Glidden, produced his own version of barbed wire with improvements which he claimed were significant enough to warrant a new patent. The patent dispute between Smith and Glidden, ultimately decided in favor of the latter in 1892, set an important precedent for US intellectual property law.

5

Bluster in Brussels

Less than a year before the outbreak of war, the belligerently incompetent German emperor Kaiser Wilhelm II blurted out an astonishing prediction (or more accurately, threat) to his royal colleague, King Albert of Belgium, during a state dinner.

On November 6, 1913, the kaiser and his retinue hosted their Belgian counterparts in Berlin for a day of royal protocol and high-level gossip, winding up with a formal ball and state dinner. As their courtiers rounded the dance floor with elegant aristocratic ladies, on the sidelines Wilhelm II and his generals plied their unsuspecting guests with champagne and thinly veiled threats, hoping to persuade (or browbeat) them into betraying Belgium's official neutrality in the event of war between Germany and France.

> "The situation is extraordinary. It is militarism run stark mad. Unless someone acting for you can bring about a different understanding, there is some day to be an awful cataclysm. No one in Europe can do it. There is too much hatred, too many jealousies."
> —*Colonel E.M. House, to President Wilson, May 1914*

This wasn't just a hypothetical scenario, according to the Germans, who cited France's new conscription law as evidence that war was inevitable. In fact, the German emperor pointed to one general, Alexander von Kluck, and bluntly told Albert, "He is the man who will lead the march on Paris." During dinner, according to the Belgian ambassador, "The Kaiser obstinately went on declaring that a conflict was inevitable and that he had no doubt of the crushing superiority of the German army." Germany's top general, Helmuth von Moltke, chimed in: "Small countries, such as Belgium, would be well advised to rally to the side of the strong if they wished to retain their independence."

These "warnings" may have helped bring about the war less than a year later. The Belgians, thoroughly rattled by the German bluster, passed the news on to the French, contributing to the hair-trigger climate in Europe. French president Raymond Poincaré later recalled "the uneasiness caused to us by King Albert's revelations as to the mind of Wilhelm II," and after the war Allied representatives at the Paris Peace Conference pointed to the dinner as proof that "several months before the crisis of July 1914 the German Kaiser had ceased to behave as an exponent of peace."

6

Hitler Was a Draft Dodger

Adolf Hitler was not the typical draft dodger. As a young man, he shirked his military duty in the Austro-Hungarian army not for any pacifist ideals but rather due to his racist beliefs.

Born in the Austrian village of Braunau am Inn in 1889, as an orphaned teenager living in Vienna Hitler came to despise the multiethnic Habsburg Empire, where German-speaking Austrians like himself had seen their power and status whittled away by other ethnic groups. The aspiring young artist and Wagner devotee also resented Emperor Franz Josef's protection of Jews threatened by the rise of anti-Semitic political parties.

Disgusted by Austria-Hungary's diversity, in May 1913 Hitler moved to Munich in the neighboring German empire (which he considered racially pure) to avoid military service in the multiethnic Habsburg armed forces. However, this wasn't exactly a foolproof plan: in January 1914 German police arrested the twenty-four-year-old artist—then living a Bohemian existence in a rundown apartment, barely supporting himself by painting tourist postcards—and bundled him off to the Austrian consulate to answer for his dereliction.

In a letter to the Austrian authorities, Hitler explained, or rather lied, that he didn't realize he was supposed to register for military service on turning age twenty. He also claimed he didn't register because he was too poor to make the trip back to Austria-Hungary (offering a choice of contradictory excuses).

Luckily for Hitler his bad diet and slovenly lifestyle combined to make him a physical wreck, and in February 1914 Austrian conscription officials judged him unfit for military duty. But this didn't mean he was opposed to military service altogether: when war broke out he enthusiastically volunteered for service in the racially pure Bavarian Army, part of the Imperial German Army.

7

Franz Ferdinand Was Killed for His Plans to Reform Austria-Hungary

The assassination of Archduke Franz Ferdinand, heir to the Habsburg throne, is still widely viewed as a desperate blow against Austro-Hungarian tyranny by Bosnian Serb nationalists—but in reality, it was motivated by fears the next emperor wasn't going to be a tyrant at all. Far from oppressing Bosnia, Archduke Franz Ferdinand was killed because his plans to reform Austria-Hungary would give more political power to Bosnian Serbs and their Slavic cousins in the empire.

Franz Ferdinand believed that Austria-Hungary's real enemies were Italy and Russia, while Serbia was ultimately a distraction. He also believed the grievances of the empire's Slavic peoples, including the Bosnian Serbs, could be resolved peacefully by making the empire into a three-way monarchy, essentially giving the Slavs their own state-within-a-state. If that didn't work, he was prepared to try an even more radical option—remaking Austria-Hungary as a federal state.

> "I will live and die for federalism; it is the sole salvation for the monarchy, if anything can save it."
> —*Archduke Franz Ferdinand, 1913*

Franz Ferdinand's plans were controversial due to opposition from the Hungarians, who stood to lose population and power if the empire created a new Slavic monarchy or transitioned to a federal government. But they also posed a threat to the ambitions of Serbian nationalists, who counted on Austrian oppression to fuel Bosnian Serb dissent; if Franz Ferdinand's planned reforms gave them self-determination inside Austria-Hungary, they might not see any reason to break away.

Dragutin Dimitrijević, code name "Apis," the ultranationalist head of Serbian military intelligence and leader of the Serbian "Black Hand" conspiracy, understood this all too well. So did the nineteen-year-old assassin, Gavrilo Princip (although his co-conspirators weren't so clear, voicing more conventional views of Franz Ferdinand as an oppressor). At his trial in October 1914, Princip stated that he killed Franz Ferdinand because, "As the future ruler [he would interfere] with our unification. He would introduce certain reforms, which, you understand, would be harmful to us."

8

The Serbian Government Warned Austria-Hungary Not to Send Franz Ferdinand

The Bosnian nationalists who assassinated Archduke Franz Ferdinand were armed (via intermediaries) by Dragutin Dimitrijević, the head of Serbian military intelligence and leader of the "Black Hand," a cabal of top military officers who controlled the civilian government of Serbia.

A constant conspirator, Dimitrijević, code name "Apis," was a true kingmaker: in 1903 he'd participated in the overthrow and brutal murder of the country's previous monarchs, the Obrenović dynasty. The new Serbian king, the mild-mannered Peter I, was understandably intimidated by Apis, while his son and heir to the throne, Alexander, was said to be in awe of the bull-necked Balkan War hero.

At the same time Dimitrijević and the Black Hand were locked in a feud with Serbia's civilian government, led by Prime Minister Nikola Pašić, the country's elder statesman. When Serbia, Bulgaria, and Greece sliced up the Ottoman Empire's Balkan territories in the First Balkan War in 1912, the Black Hand believed Serbia's civilian government betrayed the cause by allowing Bulgaria to keep land promised to Serbia. They were also upset by Pašić's attempt to reassert civilian control in the newly conquered territories. In August 1913 Dimitrijević used his connections to get himself appointed head of military intelligence, and by the summer of 1914 he was planning a coup against Pašić.

For his part Pašić, a hardened political fighter, was determined to break the power of the Black Hand. Pašić did his best to keep tabs on Apis with the help of two informants, Major Vojislav Tankosić, a partisan fighter during the Balkan Wars, and Milan Ciganović, a minor official in the Serbian state railroad. Tankosić and Ciganović kept Pašić informed of the Black Hand's coup plot and the simultaneous conspiracy to assassinate Franz Ferdinand.

In June 1914 Serbian officials tried to convince their Austrian colleagues to cancel Franz-Ferdinand's visit to Sarajevo. The Serbian ambassador to Austria-Hungary warned that it coincided with Serbia's main patriotic holiday, "Vidov Dan," which might inspire an assassination attempt. However, the warnings were vague, and Bosnia's military governor, Oskar Potiorek, assured Franz Ferdinand it was safe. Meanwhile the Serbian cabinet tried to stop the assassination plot by ordering border guards to prevent the plotters from crossing the frontier into Austrian Bosnia—but the guards were already in the grip of the Black Hand.

By now the Serbian civilian government's power struggle with the Black Hand had widened to include the monarchy. Throughout the spring of 1914 Pašić battled the Black Hand over the appointment of a new minister of war, and on June 10, 1914, King Peter, still fearful of the Black Hand, demanded that Pašić and his government resign. However, Serbia's patron Russia forced the king to reverse this unpopular decision.

Finding himself caught between Serbia's civilian government, its Russian backer, and the Black Hand, on June 24—four days before the assassination in Sarajevo—the elderly, ailing King Peter temporarily stepped down, allowing his son Alexander to reign in his place as prince regent. On his way out Peter dissolved the Serbian Parliament, triggering new elections scheduled for August 14, meaning Pašić was out in the provinces campaigning when the Austro-Hungarian ultimatum to Serbia arrived on July 24.

Too Complicated by Half:
Germany Fell Victim to Its Own Trickery

Following the assassination of Archduke Franz Ferdinand by Bosnian Serb nationalists on June 28, 1914, the leaders of Austria-Hungary—Emperor Franz Josef, Foreign Minister Count Leopold von Berchtold, and chief of the general staff Conrad von Hötzendorf—decided to settle accounts with their troublesome neighbor, the Kingdom of Serbia, once and for all.

They were urged on by Austria-Hungary's German allies, Kaiser Wilhelm II and Chancellor Bethmann-Hollweg, whose plan to crush Serbia required a big dose of deception to ensure the other Great Powers didn't interfere. Tragically this deceit backfired, leaving them victims of their own trickery.

The Germans wanted to use the assassination of Franz Ferdinand as an opportunity to break up the "Triple Entente" of Russia, France, and Britain—and the Balkan crisis seemed like the perfect wedge to drive them apart. As the traditional patron of its fellow Slavs, Russia might try to protect Serbia against Austria-Hungary, but France and Britain would be understandably reluctant to go to war over the little Balkan kingdom.

To force the Entente to a falling out, everyone first had to believe Germany had nothing to do with Austria-Hungary's plan to attack Serbia, as German involvement would rouse suspicion about their real aims. So the Germans and Austrians resorted to a ham-handed ruse in an attempt to fool the other Great Powers.

As Austria-Hungary prepared to deliver an ultimatum to Serbia on July 23, 1914, German diplomats lied to their French and British counterparts, saying they had no knowledge of its contents, including the key clauses that would force Serbia to reject the ultimatum, triggering war.

Then after the ultimatum was delivered, when their colleagues begged them to stop Austria-Hungary from declaring war on Serbia, the Germans lied again, claiming their Austro-Hungarian allies were ignoring them.

However, nobody believed Austria-Hungary would make such a momentous decision without consulting its only ally. Then, as the crisis reached its climax in the final days of July 1914, the Germans ran afoul of their own lies.

On July 28, with war looming, the British proposed a last-ditch compromise: Austria-Hungary would occupy the Serbian capital of Belgrade but leave the rest of the country untouched, giving Austria-Hungary a win while also reassuring Russia, hopefully setting the stage for negotiations. Still convinced that Britain was bluffing, German chancellor Bethmann-Hollweg promised to pass the idea along to Austria-Hungary—but secretly added that Austria-Hungary should feel free to ignore the German "advice" and proceed with the plan to crush Serbia.

This trickery would come back to haunt the Germans just one day later. After it became clear that the British might actually go to war in support of France and Russia, on the night of July 29–30 Bethmann-Hollweg frantically repeated his suggestion of a "halt in Belgrade," only this time in earnest. Of course, the Austro-Hungarians were confused, or at least acted that way: after all, the Germans had just told them to ignore the exact same suggestion the day before.

They proceeded as if they were still playing along to hoodwink the Brits, thanking their ally for the input but rebuffing the "halt in Belgrade" proposal again (in fact they may just have decided to go ahead despite Germany's cold feet). The public notices declaring general mobilization were scheduled to go up on July 31, 1914. On July 30, Tsar Nicholas II preempted the Austrian move by ordering general mobilization in Russia, setting the machinery of war in motion. The Germans' last-minute attempt to reverse course had failed, thanks to their own clumsy attempts at intrigue.

10

"Willy" and "Nicky": Wilhelm II and Tsar Nicholas II Negotiated in English

Bizarre though it may seem by modern standards, most European heads of state of the prewar years were related to each other to varying degrees, reflecting the tangled family trees of the aristocracy that had ruled the continent since medieval times. In fact, three heads of state who led their countries to war were first cousins.

King George V of Britain, Kaiser Wilhelm II of Germany, and Tsar Nicholas II of Russia were all cousins who knew each other personally from early childhood. George and Nicholas, sons of the Danish princesses Alexandra and Dagmar, became close friends and inherited their mothers' shared distrust of Germany (which had annexed the Danish province of Schleswig-Holstein in 1864). Wilhelm II, son of Victoria's eldest daughter Victoria and the short-reigning Kaiser Frederick III, remained the odd cousin out, viewed as aggressive and impulsive by the other royals. "Nicky" and "Willy" were both fluent in English, having grown up speaking it with their parents and the extended royal family.

As the diplomatic crisis resulting from the assassination of Archduke Franz Ferdinand exploded in July 1914, both monarchs felt compelled to intervene personally to try to stop the slide toward war—or at least cast blame for it on their foes in the eyes of history.

With Russia and Austria-Hungary on a collision course, and Germany secretly egging Austria-Hungary on, German chancellor Bethmann-Hollweg advised Kaiser Wilhelm II to open a direct line of communication with a personal telegram to Tsar Nicholas II, in hopes of convincing his cousin not to mobilize the Russian Army. Almost simultaneously Tsar

Nicholas II sent a personal telegram to the German emperor on the advice of Foreign Minister Sergei Sazonov.

From the beginning, neither side was fully sincere: the kaiser's assurances that he was trying to restrain Austria-Hungary were false, while the Russians may already have decided this was the moment to lunge for Constantinople, their own long-term goal. But if nothing else they both hoped to shift responsibility for the disaster onto their cousin.

In his first telegram, sent in English on July 29, 1914, at 1:00 a.m., Tsar Nicholas II (Nicky) begged his cousin, the German emperor:

> In this serious moment, I appeal to you to help me. An ignoble war has been declared to a weak country. The indignation in Russia shared fully by me is enormous. I foresee that very soon I shall be overwhelmed by the pressure forced upon me and be forced to take extreme measures which will lead to war. To try and avoid such a calamity as a European war I beg you in the name of our old friendship to do what you can to stop your allies from going too far.

Meanwhile in a message sent just a few minutes later at 1:45 a.m., also in English, Kaiser Wilhelm II (Willy) promised Nicky, "I am exerting my utmost influence to induce the Austrians to deal straightly to arrive to a satisfactory understanding with you. I confidently hope that you will help me in my efforts to smooth over difficulties that may still arise."

At this point both monarchs were conducting diplomacy ad lib, sending signals that often varied from their ambassadors' statements, probably due to genuine ignorance as well as their own desire to posture for history. These ploys to cast blame included Willy's telegram sent July 30 at 1:20 a.m. (crossing with the telegram from Nicky): "Austria has only mobilised against Servia & only a part of her army... The whole weight of the decision lies solely on you[r] shoulders now, who have to bear the responsibility for Peace or War."

On learning of Russian mobilization against Austria-Hungary, Willy melodramatically protested in another telegram on July 31, 1914: "Responsibility for the safety of my empire forces preventive measures of defence upon me. In my endeavours to maintain the peace of the world I have gone to the utmost limit possible. The responsibility for the disaster which is now threatening the whole civilized world will not be laid at my door. In this moment it still lies in your power to avert it."

Now, with war almost upon them, Nicky was equally disingenuous in his response, claiming that Russia had no aggressive intentions toward Germany and had been forced to mobilize by Austria-Hungary's own prior mobilization—one of the great lies of the First World War, as the Russian government actually ordered mobilization on July 30, a day *before* Austria-Hungary mobilized (and had implemented secret "pre-mobilization" measures as early as July 25, the day after Austria-Hungary's ultimatum to Serbia).

Still trying to shovel blame back to Willy, Nicky insisted that Russia's mobilization didn't mean war against Germany, and asked for similar assurances from Willy if Germany mobilized. However, Willy couldn't give this assurance, because Germany's mobilization plan called for an immediate attack on Russia's ally France.

In the last of the "Willy-Nicky" telegrams, sent August 1, 1914, Willy angrily blamed his cousin for failing to halt Russian mobilization, forcing Germany's hand: "I yesterday pointed out to your government the way by which alone war may be avoided. Although I requested an answer for noon today, no telegram from my ambassador conveying an answer from your Government has reached me as yet. I therefore have been obliged to mobilise my army."

PART 2

1914: Out of the Blue

IN AUGUST 1914 Germany attacked France through Belgium, aiming to either encircle the French Army or break the French fortress line from behind—but whatever the plan was, it failed at the First Battle of the Marne, forcing the Germans to retreat to northern France, where both sides dug in, inaugurating trench warfare. Here the small British Expeditionary Force would play a key role holding off the last German attempt to break through Allied defense at the First Battle of Ypres in October–December 1914.

Meanwhile to the south, France attacked Germany directly across their common border in August, in hopes of liberating the "lost provinces" of Alsace-Lorraine—but suffered a bloody defeat in the Battle of the Frontiers, with 27,000 French soldiers killed on one day alone (August 22, still remembered as the bloodiest day in French history).

On the Eastern Front, the Germans were shocked by how fast the Russians mobilized, scrambling to defend East Prussia against two Russian armies. The German generals Paul von Hindenburg and Erich Ludendorff turned the tables with a stunning victory at the Battle of Tannenberg. They immediately faced an even bigger challenge with the collapse of their ally Austria-Hungary's armies before the

"Russian steamroller" in Austrian Galicia. Worse still, Austria-Hungary suffered an even more embarrassing defeat at the hands of tiny Serbia at the Battle of Kolubara in November–December 1914.

Despite these setbacks Germany and Austria-Hungary got a big boost in November 1914, when the leaders of the Ottoman Empire decided to join the "Central Powers" in hopes of reversing their own empire's long-term decline. War Minister Enver Pasha took the Ottoman Empire into war without consulting the rest of the Ottoman cabinet (mostly fellow members of the Committee of Union and Progress, known as the "Young Turks") with some help from the German ships *Goeben* and *Breslau*. The addition of the Ottoman Empire to the Central Powers forced the Allies to fight on new fronts in the Middle East and Caucasus, promising an even longer war.

As 1914 drew to a close, there was a famous moment of good cheer with the Christmas Eve Truce, when ordinary soldiers on the Western Front left their trenches to fraternize with the enemy in no man's land. But the war had only just begun.

H.G. Wells Coined the Phrase "The War That Will End War"

In the decades before the Great War many believed war had become impossible in the modern era, because it would be so destructive to both sides. But that didn't prevent war from breaking out, raising some unsettling questions. Was humanity hopelessly irrational and doomed to self-inflicted suffering?

In response, writers and public intellectuals on both sides tried to find meaning in the war that would somehow justify its horror—themes that were swiftly adopted as part of official propaganda. In Germany, for example, intellectuals justified the war as a defense of the country's unique *kultur* ("Germanic civilization"), while Italian nationalists like the journalist and soldier Benito Mussolini presented the war as a sacred quest to "redeem" Italy.

> "They think that the war is over!
> Only the dead have seen the end of war."
> —*George Santayana, 1922*

One of the most popular rationales was first formulated by the celebrated British futurist and science fiction author H.G. Wells, in "The War That Will End War," a commentary first published in *The Daily News* on August 14, 1914. Wells argued that the war had resulted from German militarism, which had to be destroyed:

This is already the vastest war in history. It is a war not of nations, but of mankind. It is a war to exorcise a world-madness and end an age... For this is now a war for peace. It aims straight at disarmament. It aims at a settlement that shall stop this sort of thing for ever. Every soldier who fights against Germany now is a crusader against war. This, the greatest of all wars, is not just another war—it is the last war!

The phrase would go on to see a number of variations, including the version popularized by President Woodrow Wilson: "I promise you that this will be the final war—the war to end all wars." Later the phrase acquired a sardonic overtone, reflecting the dashed hopes of idealists as the immediate "postwar" years turned out to be anything but, and the new League of Nations proved powerless to stop the bloodshed.

12

Germany's "Hymn of Hate"

Few cultural artifacts of the First World War can convey the sense of bloodcurdling hatred that prevailed on both sides better than Germany's "Hymn of Hate." After trying to enlist but being turned away as unfit for service, in August 1914, the German-Jewish poet Ernst Lissauer wrote his notorious poem, "Hymn of Hate Against England," which invoked German unity against the deceitful English.

The poem's rabid nationalism was fully in line with Lissauer's background as an assimilated German Jew; as the German artist Stefan Zweig observed of the poet, "Like many Jews, he believed in Germany more fervently than the most fervent German." Not coincidentally, Lissauer also coined the German Army slogan *"Gott strafe England,"* "May God punish England."

> "You will we hate with a lasting hate,
> We will never forego our hate,
> Hate by water and hate by land,
> Hate of the head and hate of the hand,
> Hate of the hammer and hate of the crown,
> Hate of seventy millions, choking down.
> We love as one, we hate as one,
> We have one foe and one alone—
> England!"
> —*Ernst Lissauer, "Hymn of Hate Against England"*

Arriving amid cresting patriotic fervor, the "Hymn of Hate" enjoyed runaway popularity in 1914, with Zweig later recalling, "The poem fell like a shell into a munitions depot." Along with the slogan *"Gott strafe England,"* the poem became one of the most recognizable expressions of German nationalism and anti-British feeling during the war.

While German liberals criticized the poem, it was in line with the German military's agenda. In October 1914, German Sixth Army Commander Prince Rupprecht of Bavaria ordered the "Hymn of Hate" distributed to all the troops under his command as they were about to attack the English at Ypres, with the comment: "Take revenge upon them, for they are our worst enemies!" In 1915 Lissauer received the Order of the Red Eagle from Kaiser Wilhelm II for his literary contributions to the war effort, though he later said he regretted writing the poem and refused to allow it to be reproduced in school textbooks.

13

Both Sides Banned "Enemy" Music

The Germans weren't the only ones indulging in an over-the-top hate fest: governments and patriotic civilians on both sides went to absurd lengths to demonstrate their hatred of the enemy, often in petty ways—like banning music by "enemy composers."

On August 15, 1914, the planners of Britain's Promenade Concerts removed all living German composers from the program at the request of the music publisher paying for the festival. The problem was banning all German, Austrian, and Hungarian music would mean removing Bach, Mozart, Beethoven, Haydn, Brahms, Mendelssohn, Schubert, Schumann, Liszt, Wagner, Bruckner, and Mahler, among others. So the Promenade Concert organizers settled on banning living composers, like Richard Strauss, who were said to represent German militarism.

> "I may not be a first-rate composer,
> but I am a first-class second-rate composer."
> —*Richard Strauss*

In France the National League for the Defense of French Music demanded a total ban on German and Austrian music, including the greats, but French orchestras opted for the more moderate ban on living composers while allowing popular favorites. However, as the war went on some of the most famous German composers were rejected on ideological grounds, with Mozart, Schubert, Handel, Haydn, and Wagner all banned because of supposed anti-French or Germanic sentiment (on the other hand Beethoven was safely, if improbably, classified as Belgian due to his Flemish grandfather).

Other combatants went further, at least on paper: Germany banned all Italian opera in 1915 in revenge for Italy's "betrayal" of the Triple Alliance, and in November 1916 the Italian government banned all music by Austrian and German composers, of any era, for the duration of the war. But musicians were sometimes reluctant to endorse bans on enemy composers, reasoning that artists weren't responsible for crimes committed by their countrymen (especially when they had been dead for decades). At a concert in Rome in 1916 the legendary conductor Arturo Toscanini, though a fierce Italian patriot, defiantly closed the performance with a piece by Wagner, arousing hecklers in the audience.

The United States was also swept up in the composer-banning craze. In October 1917 the New York City Board of Education banned German operas from musical instruction in public schools (doubtless winning a round of applause from students), and a month later the Pittsburgh Orchestra Association banned "all music written by any German composer, and all music by a subject of any of Germany's allies." Though not quite as extreme, in 1918 the New York Philharmonic and New York Metropolitan Opera banned all music by living German composers. Karl Muck, the German-born Swiss conductor of the Boston Symphony, was interned after a fabricated story that he refused to conduct "The Star-Spangled Banner" (in fact the symphony board never asked him to).

However, soldiers at the front drew solace from the beauty of classical music regardless of nationality. In April 1915 an anonymous French officer wrote that to pass the time, "my fellow non-commissioned officers and I began humming the nine symphonies of Beethoven. I cannot tell what a thrill those notes woke within us…" A British officer, Stanley Spencer, recounted that he and a companion "spent part of the night in cheering each other up and passing the time by whistling or humming such pieces as we could remember… It is unlikely that Mendelssohn's 'Spring Song' and Rachmaninoff's 'Third Prelude' have ever been heard under more strange or unpleasant conditions."

14

German Troops Fought Allies in Asia and Africa

Although most of the fighting took place in Europe, the First World War was exactly that—a global conflict, with action in far-flung theaters.

Tsingtao. The Germans seized the territory of Tsingtao on China's Shandong Peninsula in 1897, forcing the Qing Dynasty's mandarins to give them a long-term lease for the Kiautschou (Jiaozhou) Bay concession. Hoping to create a naval outpost in the Far East, Germany built an orderly German colony on top of the old Chinese fishing village of Tsingtao. After war broke out, Japanese imperialists coveted the German naval base, which would give them a foothold in China.

On August 23, 1914, Japan declared war on Germany after it refused to give up Tsingtao. The ensuing siege from August 27–November 7, 1914, saw the German territory cut off by overwhelming Japanese and British forces, including a joint naval blockade and trenches on the land side. The siege finally ended when Japanese troops overwhelmed the roughly 5,000 German defenders, who went on to four years' imprisonment in Japan. The Siege of Tsingtao also featured history's first known attempt at air-sea warfare with an unsuccessful bomb attack by a Japanese seaplane against German and Austro-Hungarian vessels.

Pacific Islands and Papua New Guinea. Toward the end of the nineteenth century German imperialists, getting a late start in the colonial game, scrambled to expand their holdings wherever they could—which included protectorates over Pacific territories in the Solomon Islands, Caroline Islands, Marianas, and Samoa, as well as a large chunk of what is now Papua New Guinea (imaginatively named Kaiser-Wilhelms-Land).

On the declaration of war Japan and Australia both lunged for the German territories. After overrunning German territory on the New Guinea mainland in August and September 1914, the Australians encountered resistance at the Battle of Bita Paka on the neighboring island of Neu Pommern (later New Britain). Here an enemy force of around 50 German officers and 240 native troops forced a much larger Australian force to lay siege to a radio tower, used to communicate with German commerce raiders in the Pacific, before surrendering on September 11, 1914. However, German-led native troops then held out for four days at the Siege of Toma on September 14–17.

To the north the Japanese had a relatively easy time seizing control of Germany's sparsely populated Pacific Island territories, which the League of Nations formally ceded to Japan after the war as the South Pacific Mandate in 1919.

German East Africa (Tanzania). The most impressive guerrilla warfare campaign of the war was fought in German East Africa (today Tanzania), where a small number of German and native troops outfought and eluded much larger British, Belgian, and Portuguese colonial forces sent to hunt them down.

Germany had taken control of East Africa, around three times the size of Germany, in 1885, and on the eve of war there were just 5,000 Europeans versus 7.5 million natives. However, over four and a half years, the German commander, General Paul Emil von Lettow-Vorbeck, led his mixed force of 12,000 African askaris and 3,500 European soldiers on an incredible trek across East African jungle, savannah, deserts, and swamps, carrying out ambushes and destroying railroads.

Contrary to racist stereotypes, the askaris were highly trained soldiers who displayed remarkable loyalty to the German cause. Hundreds of askaris fought to the bitter end, which meant marching across thousands of miles before Lettow-Vorbeck finally surrendered, undefeated, to British forces in what is now Mbala, Zambia, on November 25, 1918 (two weeks after the war ended in Europe).

German Southwest Africa (Namibia). German Southwest Africa (today Namibia) had been the scene of a genocide before the war: in 1904–1907 the Germans had punished a native rebellion by attempting to exterminate the Herero, Nama, and San peoples, killing up to 100,000.

In 1915 South African and British troops invaded German Southwest Africa from the land and sea, with amphibious landings at the ports of Lüderitzbucht and Swakopmund in January, followed by ground forces crossing the Orange River in April. The colonial capital, Windhoek (site of a huge German radio transmitter), fell to the South Africans in May, and the last German and colonial troops surrendered on July 8, 1915.

Kamerun (Cameroon). Another colony acquired in 1884, Kamerun (today Cameroon) was even more sparsely populated than Germany's other African territories. The local colonial government put up a good fight thanks to well-trained and disciplined native troops, who fought British troops from Nigeria and French troops from the Congo for over a year and a half. At the Siege of Mora in northern Kamerun, just over 200 German and native troops held out from August 1914 until February 1916, holed up on a mountain, until starvation forced them to surrender. Meanwhile most of the rest of the German and native troops escaped Kamerun and went into internment in the neighboring Spanish-controlled territory of Río Muni.

Togoland. The smallest of all Germany's African territories, Togoland was also the fastest to fall to Allied troops. After the war broke out, a force of about 1,000 native and German police and paramilitary units retreated from the capital, Lomé, to the northern town of Kamina, in an attempt to defend a high-powered radio transmitter connecting Germany to commerce raiders in the South Atlantic. A series of fierce rearguard actions, skirmishes, and raids ended at the Battle of Chra, where British and French forces trapped the Germans on August 22–23, 1914. After demolishing the radio towers the German forces finally surrendered on August 26, 1914.

15

When Generals Collapse

As his name suggests, Helmuth von Moltke "The Younger" had a superb pedigree: his uncle Helmuth von Moltke "The Elder" was the architect of Prussia's victories over Austria, Denmark, and France in the wars of German unification from 1866–1871. After serving as an assistant to his uncle, Moltke became aide-de-camp to Kaiser Wilhelm II, then rose swiftly through the ranks to become chief of the German general staff on the retirement of Alfred von Schlieffen in 1906.

> "We are ready. The sooner, the better."
> —*Helmuth von Moltke "The Younger," June 1914*

As Germany's top general, Moltke was responsible for the execution of Germany's war plan in 1914 but soon started to crack under pressure. Already high strung, he burst into tears on the evening of August 1, when Kaiser Wilhelm II casually ordered an impossible last-minute improvisation for war against Russia but not France (soon rendered irrelevant by events). By Moltke's own account his nerves were "shattered"—and an even bigger psychological meltdown was looming.

Unnerved by the surprisingly rapid Russian advance in East Prussia, Moltke shifted several more army corps to the Eastern Front, further weakening the right wing. As a result, in the critical days of August and September 1914 the Germans failed to envelop the French Army or breach the French fortress line—whichever the main goal was. This left the German First Army's right flank exposed to the French garrison in Paris as the German armies pivoted south. Meanwhile the French chief of the general staff, Joseph Joffre, was rapidly forming the new French Sixth Army northeast of Paris with troops transferred by rail from other parts of the front (some famously delivered to the front by a fleet of Parisian motor taxis).

Now the whole German campaign started to unravel, along with Moltke's sanity. On September 5–6, 1914, the new French Sixth Army under General Michel-Joseph Manoury clashed with the German First Army at the Battle of the Ourcq. Calling off the pursuit of the battered BEF, First Army commander Alexander von Kluck ordered two army corps to reverse direction and march north to protect the German flank.

As the German First Army pivoted to face the new threat north of Paris, the neighboring Second Army under Karl von Bülow continued attacking south, opening a dangerous gap in the German line—but the commanders failed to communicate and the gap only grew wider. By September 8 the situation of the German armies in northern France was critical, as the BEF and French Fifth Army advanced toward the opening in the German line, raising the prospect of breakthrough and defeat.

At the moment of supreme decision Moltke suffered fatal indecision. Isolated at supreme headquarters in Luxembourg, on the morning of September 8 he made what is still one of the most controversial decisions of the war. He sent a relatively junior officer, Major Richard Hentsch, on an extraordinary mission—visit the German armies in the field, make an appraisal of the situation, and order a general retreat if necessary.

Over the next two days Hentsch embarked on a breakneck 400-mile car trip, gathering facts that painted a very alarming picture. On the evening of September 8, 1914, Second Army commander Bülow told Hentsch he believed a general retreat was necessary. The next morning Hentsch proceeded to the First Army, where von Kluck's chief of staff disclosed they already had contingency plans for retreat, even though von

Kluck was planning to attack the French Sixth Army and believed victory was still possible. That afternoon Hentsch sent a message to headquarters recommending a general withdrawal to a shorter, more defensible line to the north on September 10—stopping von Kluck at the decisive moment.

Historians still debate whether Hentsch overstepped his authority, but the 40-mile gap between the First and Second Armies was real enough, and in any event Germany's top general had now suffered complete mental collapse. Pacing frantically and showing signs of paranoia, Moltke was obviously no longer in control of the situation. The German Army was leaderless as it withdrew north to the Aisne River and dug in (the start of trench warfare). Faced with the long-feared two-front conflict against France and Russia, Moltke supposedly told Kaiser Wilhelm II, "Majesty, we have lost the war!"

His colleagues on the general staff recognized that Moltke, broken by Germany's defeat at the Marne, was no longer fit to command the German Army. On September 14, 1914, he resigned as chief of the general staff and was replaced by Erich von Falkenhayn. Moltke never recovered, dying of a stroke in 1916.

Marie Curie Invented Mobile X-Ray Machines

One of the most famous female scientists in history, Madame Marie Curie put her discoveries to work for her adopted homeland, France, with the invention of mobile X-ray machines that saved thousands of French soldiers' lives on the Western Front—no thanks to the French government.

When war broke out Curie, co-discoverer of radium with her husband Pierre in 1898, went to French authorities with a proposal for compact mobile X-ray machines in the back of vans, which could easily visit field hospitals close to the front, allowing surgeons to locate bullets, shrapnel, and broken bones in wounded soldiers. When the French Army dragged its feet, the Union of Women of France agreed to fund the project, but some technical hurdles remained.

The main challenge was finding a way to power the X-ray units. Since there was no reliable source of electricity at the front, Curie modified vans by adding dynamos to the engines, converting them into generators that powered the X-rays directly (most vehicles were still hand-cranked, and car batteries for electric starters weren't widely used until 1920). Curie worked with remarkable speed: the first "radiological car" went into service at the "Miracle on the Marne" in early September, just one month after the war started.

> "One never notices what has been done;
> one can only see what remains to be done."
> —*Marie Curie*

With her concept proved, in the fall of 1914 Curie made the rounds begging rich Frenchwomen to donate new or used vehicles—surely a trial for the extremely shy scientist, who preferred the solitude of her lab (separately Curie tried to donate her two gold Nobel Prizes to the war effort, but bank officials refused to melt them down).

While scraping together a fleet of twenty cars and vans, Curie and her daughter Irène also gave a crash course in radiology to her all-female team of volunteers, covering physics, human anatomy, and the fine points of developing film in the vehicles' small, cramped darkrooms. By the end of the war the Curies trained more than 150 women to operate the X-ray machines, and the Nobel laureate herself learned to drive (as well as change flat tires and repair carburetors) so she could operate her own "little Curie."

By the end of the year Curie's X-ray vans were in service up and down the Western Front. Over the course of the war over a million French and Allied soldiers received X-rays from the mobile vans.

The hastily improvised mobile X-ray vehicles had scant safety features, meaning that many of the operators were probably exposed to dangerous levels of X-rays. Curie herself later attributed her own illness with aplastic anemia, which resulted in her death in 1934, to her wartime work with the X-ray vans.

17

Flooding Flanders

After Germany's failed invasion of northern France, Belgium became the finish line for the dramatic (though misnamed) "Race to the Sea," when Allied and German armies tried to outflank each other north from the Aisne River, leaving behind two lines of trenches stretching all the way to the English Channel. The Germans mounted one last attempt to break through the Allied lines in Flanders at the First Battle of Ypres from October 19–November 30, 1914. With the German Fourth Army threatening to pour across the Yser River north of Ypres, it was crucial for the Allies to shorten their line so they could concentrate their available troops farther south, around Ypres itself. Fortunately, there was a straightforward, if drastic, solution.

As fighting raged from the North Sea beaches to Ypres, on October 21, 1914, a Belgian officer, Lieutenant General Émile Dossin, ordered a local tug skipper to open the sluice gates protecting the low-lying country around Nieuport. By the following day the rising waters had flooded around four square kilometers, temporarily protecting Nieuport from the German advance.

Inspired by this local success, on October 25, 1914, a Belgian staff officer, Prudent Nuyten, suggested that King Albert order the full-scale inundation of the floodplains around the river. The king immediately agreed to this measure, which first required blocking a number of railroad culverts to keep the water from pouring into the rest of Belgium.

On October 27–29, while Allied forces withdrew behind the railroad embankment, German troops approaching from the east suddenly found themselves knee- and then waist-deep in brackish water filled with human corpses and dead horses, among other debris. Five German divisions beat a hasty retreat to higher ground to the east, and both sides watched as a long, shallow lake rose between them.

"You are standing by the edge of what appears to be a mighty lake, the silver waters of which stretch far away into the distance. A light breeze plays upon the surface, darkening it here and there and causing little waves to rise like sword gleams under the moonlight... But as you stand entranced by this vision there comes to your nostrils a terrible taint of death that robs the scene of all its illusion of peace and beauty."
—*Wilson McNair*

The Belgians ultimately submerged an area around 15 kilometers long and 3–5 kilometers wide under 3 feet of water. The inundation made infantry operations impossible, and would remain in place for the duration of the war; during cold winter months the Allies shelled the ice to break it up and prevent a German crossing.

Britain's Bantam Battalions

When war broke out in August 1914, the all-volunteer British Army numbered around 250,000, and the United Kingdom was able to dispatch just six divisions—four infantry and two cavalry—for service in the British Expeditionary Force (BEF) in France. By comparison its new ally France mobilized ninety-three divisions, France's ally Russia ninety-eight, and foe Germany 103.

In the weeks following Germany's invasion of Belgium, the small but proud BEF was bled white by steady attrition at the battles of Mons, Le Cateau, the Marne, the Aisne, and Arras. As trench warfare unfolded through northern France and Belgium all the way to the North Sea, the Allies fended off a final German attempt to break through to the English Channel thanks in large part to the grit of the battered BEF at the First Battle of Ypres.

The Old Contemptibles

In an infamous order of the day, issued on August 19, 1914, Kaiser Wilhelm II ordered his soldiers to destroy Britain's "contemptible little army." This prompted the members of the original British Expeditionary Force to adopt the defiant nickname "The Old Contemptibles."

By the end of 1914 the BEF had suffered over 100 percent casualties, meaning a large proportion of its ranks had already been replaced several times over by fresh troops drawn from regimental establishments at home.

Britain needed more troops, fast. But British politicians, proud of their tradition of strictly voluntary military service, were reluctant to resort to a draft. Until January 1916, when Britain finally adopted conscription, the United Kingdom relied on cleverly crafted appeals to patriotism and a number of recruiting schemes to drive enlistment.

The best-known gimmick was the "pals" battalions, which promised that men who signed up together would be allowed to serve together— encouraging friends and groups such as neighbors, coworkers, clubs, and sports teams to enlist at the same time.

Another recruitment scheme was the "bantam battalions"—units formed entirely of men under the army's standard minimum height requirement of 5'3", compared to an average male height of 5'6" at the time. Facing daunting manpower demands, Secretary of War Lord Kitchener embraced the idea of special battalions composed of short men at the suggestion of a member of Parliament, Alfred Bigland. Bigland was moved by the case of a miner rejected because he was 5'2" (who supposedly vowed to fight anyone who mentioned the missing inch).

There was still a minimum height requirement of 5', and recruits had to have a chest circumference of 34" to join the bantam battalions, where they served under officers of ordinary height. Overall around 30,000 men joined the British Army through one of twenty-nine bantam battalions, most fighting bravely alongside their taller companions. However, during the Battle of the Somme, 1916, problems with discipline and the difficulty of finding suitable recruits to replace casualties led the army to dissolve the bantam battalions, which were merged with other units.

19

Italy Switched Sides (Slowly)

In 1882 the Kingdom of Italy, worried about France's long history of meddling and Russian ambitions in the Balkans, joined the Triple Alliance with Germany and Austria-Hungary, a defensive agreement to ward off the threats to east and west. But the alliance with Austria-Hungary was awkward to say the least, because the Habsburg Empire continued to rule a large population of ethnic Italians in the Trentino and Trieste, which Italian nationalists openly claimed for Italy. For his part Archduke Franz Ferdinand, heir to the Habsburg throne, wanted to reclaim provinces lost to Italy during the Austro-Prussian War in 1866.

Despite warming relations with France, Italy continued to adhere to the Triple Alliance—and while Italian nationalists viewed Austria-Hungary as the enemy, the Italian general staff dutifully carried out their responsibilities in military planning with their Austro-Hungarian and German counterparts.

In January 1913 the allies agreed that, in case of war with France, Italy would send five army corps to serve in western Germany, and at a meeting in October 1913 Italy's top general, Alberto Pollio, impressed his German and Austrian counterparts with his commitment to the alliance. Planning continued into the next spring: in March 1914 General Luigi Zuccari visited Berlin to draw up plans to send the Italian Third Army to serve in Germany's Rhine region in case of war, dispatching three Italian army corps and two cavalry divisions via Austria.

But political and diplomatic events were already taking a very different course. In August 1913 the Austrian governor of Trieste angered Italy with the Hohenlohe Decrees, formalizing discrimination against ethnic

Italians in the empire. Then during the Balkan Wars Italy clashed with Austria-Hungary over its aggressive stance toward Serbia.

After receiving their copy of Austria-Hungary's ultimatum to Serbia on July 24, Italian Foreign Minister San Giuliano and Prime Minister Salandra immediately decided Italy didn't have to join Austria-Hungary since it had failed to consult Italy about its war plans as required under the terms of the defensive Triple Alliance. They also reminded Austria-Hungary and Germany of Italy's right to "territorial compensation" in case Austria-Hungary conquered Serbia.

Once again, military preparations had nothing to do with the fast-unraveling diplomatic situation. On July 31, King Victor Emmanuel's council of ministers voted in favor of maintaining Italian neutrality in the impending war. German and Austrian politicians huffed about Italy's "betrayal," and Italian public opinion took a sharp anti-Austrian turn, whipped up by nationalist newspapers, as all eyes turned to Italy's "lost" provinces in the north.

And then, in typical fashion, nothing happened, as the Italians spent the better part of a year arguing about what to do. Through the fall and winter of 1914–1915, "Interventionists" like the rabble-rousing nationalist journalist Benito Mussolini called for Italy to declare war on Austria to "redeem" the lost provinces, leading to violent clashes with anti-war socialists.

Finally, a concerted campaign of propaganda and bribery, paid for largely by French and British intelligence, managed to sway enough Italian politicians to get a declaration of war on Austria-Hungary through Parliament on May 21, 1915. However, Italy failed to declare war on Germany or the Ottoman Empire, and its lackluster military performance gave the Allies an excuse to break their promise and give some territory earmarked for Italy to the new Yugoslav state after the war instead.

20

Germany's Jihad

Among the many eccentric vanities of Kaiser Wilhelm II, perhaps the oddest was that he viewed himself as the protector of the world's Muslims, even though he was a Christian.

Heavily colored by Europe's "Orientalist" tradition presenting romantic views of "the East," the German emperor's infatuation with Islam dated back to his famous 1898 visit to Constantinople, capital of the Ottoman Empire, when he proclaimed himself a friend to 300 million Muslims around the world. Of course, it was no coincidence that most of his new Muslim friends lived in the British, French, or Russian colonial empires.

> "…if I had come there without any religion at all I would
> certainly have turned Mahommetan!"
> —*Kaiser Wilhelm II, letter to Tsar Nicholas II, 1898*

With war looming, the German emperor first vowed to start a worldwide Islamic revolution at a secret meeting in Potsdam with his crown council on July 30, 1914. The idea wasn't as crazy as it might seem, given Germany's alliance with the Muslim Ottoman Empire, secretly signed three days later. The Ottoman sultans claimed the title of caliph, or leader of the world's Muslim community, giving them the power to declare holy war, and the feeble Sultan Mehmed V was already under the thumb of the Committee of Union and Progress (CUP or "Young Turk") triumvirate led by war minister Enver Pasha.

On November 14, 1914, the Ottoman Empire's Sheikh-ul-Islam, or top religious authority, declared a "Cihad-ı Mukaddes" or "holy war" against the empire's enemies. The *fatwa* or "religious decree" stated that it was the "a religious duty for [Muslims] to declare war against Russia, Britain, and France and their helpers and supporters, who are enemies of the Islamic Caliphate and trying to—may God forbid—extinguish the divine light of Islam by attacking the seat of the Caliph and the Ottoman nation with battleships and land forces." There were some awkward issues surrounding the jihad, beginning with the fact that its main sponsors, Germany and Austria-Hungary, were also Christian infidels, but this was overlooked for obvious reasons.

As it turned out, the German jihad was neither "holy" nor much of a "war." One of the more ambitious attempts was the expedition by German Army officers Oskar Niedermayer and Werner Otto von Hentig to Afghanistan in 1915–1916, a vain effort to persuade the Afghan emir Habibullah Khan to join the Central Powers, coinciding with German attempts to win over neighboring Persia. However, British intelligence captured operatives and intercepted secret communications across Europe and Asia to neutralize the threat.

The Germans and Turks had more success inciting a rebellion by the Muslim Senussi tribes, former Ottoman vassals, in the desert region straddling Italian Libya and British Egypt. The rebellion lasted from January 1915 to November 1918, but as in the Niedermayer-Hentig expedition, geographic barriers and Allied control of the Mediterranean prevented the Central Powers from delivering much in the way of weapons or supplies (although a German agent, Edgar Pröbster, twice succeeded in delivering cash after landing on the Libyan coast by submarine).

Elsewhere a mutiny by Muslim Indian sepoys stationed in Singapore in February 1915 was attributed at least partly to the influence of German propaganda and alleged incitement by a German agent. The mutiny was crushed with the execution of forty-seven mutineers, and the incident ultimately prompted the formation of British Criminal Intelligence, better known as Special Branch, in 1919.

However, a more typical result of the German jihad was the case of Max Roloff, who presented himself to German spymasters as a journalist with Middle Eastern expertise, then supposedly went to Mecca disguised as a Muslim pilgrim in December 1914, in order to recruit rebels to destabilize Egypt and other Allied possessions. Actually, Roloff was just a con man who just took the money and lived a comfortable life in Holland, making up stories about his Arabian adventures that he eventually published in Germany. Ironically his fictional tales of traveling to Mecca as a nonbeliever, in violation of the holy laws governing the shrine, damaged Turkish-German relations as well as Germany's reputation with the Muslims it was supposedly trying to help.

Women Shamed Men Into Enlisting with White Feathers

Although some pundits have credited women with more pacifist instincts than men, there were plenty of fire-breathing women in the First World War. Before Britain adopted the draft in 1916, one contingent of patriotic (and rather judgmental) women set out to shame civilian men into joining the army voluntarily by handing out white feathers in public—a symbol of cowardice.

The "Order of the White Feather" was a patriotic, shame-based organization, founded by the retired Admiral Charles Fitzgerald and Mrs. Humphrey Ward, a popular author, amid growing concern about the British Army's looming manpower shortage. Fitzgerald launched the organization by personally deputizing thirty women in Folkestone to hand out feathers to any man not in uniform in public.

Sometimes the feathers were attached to burrs and thrown or surreptitiously placed, only to be discovered later (after pointing and laughter). Young women were encouraged to "cut" shirkers from their company, meaning romantically. British War Secretary Lord Kitchener, who endorsed the white feather campaign, stated: "The women could play a great part in the emergency by using their influence with their husbands and sons to take their proper share in the country's defence, and every girl who had a sweetheart should tell men that she would not walk out with him again until he had done his part in licking the Germans."

However, the white feather plan had some obvious holes: for one thing, there were several million workers who worked in war industries and still wore civilian clothes. In response, workers in war industries began wearing a badge with the slogan "King and Country" to let would-be shamers know they were serving too. Meanwhile the writer Compton Mackenzie complained that "idiotic young women were using white feathers to get rid of boyfriends of whom they were tired."

"To the young women of London: Is your 'Best Boy' wearing Khaki? If not don't YOU THINK he should be? If your young man neglects his duty to his King and Country, the time may come when he will NEGLECT YOU!"
—*Wartime poster*

Soldiers also complained of receiving a white feather while in civilian attire. In one of the most egregious cases, on October 12, 1915, a woman gave a white feather to Royal Navy Seaman George Samson, who had just received the Victoria Cross for bravery during the disastrous Gallipoli landings, when he saved dozens of wounded under enemy fire while badly wounded himself. Another soldier, Private Harold Carter, was publicly abused by a Royal Navy officer while in civilian clothes in front of a music hall: "He made me feel about as big as a worm. I just sat there on my own while people looked at me. I should like to have jumped up and told them I'd just come out of the trenches at Ypres, but I couldn't. I came out disgusted and went home."

Boys still underage also received white feathers, driving some of them to sign up illegally. James Lovegrove, sixteen years old, was verbally attacked by a group of women on his way to work: "They started shouting and yelling at me, calling me all sorts of names for not being a soldier! Do you know what they did? They stuck a white feather in my coat, meaning I was a coward. Oh, I did feel dreadful, so ashamed. I went to the recruiting office."

Widespread criticism of the campaign for these and other reasons led to a backlash against the white feather distributors. Later some pacifist groups cheekily adopted white feathers as a sign of peace.

22

Banning Booze Didn't Help

Alcohol was the bane of military and civilian authorities during the First World War, lowering military effectiveness and industrial productivity, prompting most combatant nations to crack down on booze. But dedicated soldiers and civilians could usually find a way to get their hands on some anyway.

As Russia mobilized on July 31, 1914, the tsarist regime introduced a sweeping ban on the production and sale of vodka, the national spirit. This had a big impact on state finances, as revenues derived from the sales duty on vodka contributed up to 40 percent of the Russian government's prewar income. Moreover, it drove production underground, according to John Morse, an Englishman serving with the Russian Army, who wrote in 1915 that, "whatever the edicts of the Czar, this fiery liquor was always plentiful enough amongst the soldiers and the peasants..."

In December 1914 the Imperial German Army banned alcohol for all troops in the field, and in April 1915 the German government limited beer production. Civilians complained about watered-down brew, but the rules don't seem to have prevented alcohol from finding its way to soldiers.

Britain took action as well—though some of it was symbolic. In the first Defense of the Realm Act, passed in September 1914, Parliament restricted the business hours of pubs, and in 1915 the Welsh politician David Lloyd George implored workers to cut back, while King George V announced the British royal family would abstain from alcohol for the duration. However, alcohol consumption actually seemed to be increasing, thanks to the rising wages of industrial workers. In summer 1916 the British government resorted to more severe measures, seizing control of breweries and pubs in northern England and Scotland, watering down beer, and banning alcohol advertising.

Pubs in the War

Pubs and other venues seized by the British government during the First World War continued to operate as official establishments, staffed by government employees, until 1971.

For most of the war a public debate raged in Britain about whether troops should have alcohol, pitting teetotalers (often religiously inspired) against those who favored a tipple. In the face of opposition from Christian temperance advocates, many British soldiers and officers defended the use of rum as a pick-me-up and painkiller in the trenches.

Alcohol undoubtedly offered a temporary coping mechanism—although a double-edged one—to officers and men enduring the horrors of war and the elements. The British poet and novelist Robert Graves remembered the Battle of Loos in fall 1915: "From the morning of September 24th to the night October 3rd, I had in all eight hours of sleep. I kept myself awake and alive by drinking about a bottle of whiskey a day. I had never drunk it before, and have seldom drunk it since; it certainly helped me then." However, Graves noted that some of his peers went overboard: "The unfortunates were officers who had endured two years or more of continuous trench service… I knew three or four who had worked up to the point of two bottles of whiskey a day before being lucky enough to get wounded or sent home in some other way."

23

France Ran Officially Sanctioned Brothels

The French nation's legendarily frank, practical view of sex and romance was on full display during the First World War, when the military established a whole network of officially sanctioned brothels, open to French and Allied soldiers alike.

Reasoning that it would be easier to perform check-ups for sexually transmitted diseases on soldiers and prostitutes in official establishments, the French government licensed a total of 137 official brothels in thirty-five big towns over the course of the war. Separate brothels were established for officers and enlisted men, the former distinguished by blue lamps, the latter with red.

It's hard to know exactly how many prostitutes worked as employees of the French government, but the number was probably in the tens of thousands, given the traffic: a British government study found that 171,000 men visited brothels over a fifty-seven-week period beginning in 1915 in the French port of Le Havre alone. To this must be added an unknown number of unlicensed brothels and solo sex workers, again surely in the thousands.

One French physician, Dr. Léon Bizard, recalled a full workday for prostitutes in the official brothels: "You could find anything you wanted in the brothels in the surrounding area and at the camps. It was a mêlée, a hard, dangerous and disgusting business. Fifty, sixty, up to a hundred men of all colours and races to see every day, all under the constant threat of air raids and bombardments."

Given their circumstances, it wasn't hard to see why soldiers ignored the injunctions to abstinence. As the poet and novelist Robert Graves explained: "There were no restraints in France; these boys had money to spend and knew that they stood a good chance of being killed within a few weeks anyhow. They did not want to die virgins."

One British soldier, a Corporal Wood, described a familiar scene in front of a French brothel: "There was a great crowd of fellows, four or five deep and about 30 yards in length, waiting just like a crowd waiting for a football cup tie in Blighty. It was half an hour before opening time, so we had to see the opening ceremony. At about five minutes to six, the lamp was lit. To the minute, at six the door was opened. Then commenced the crush to get in."

Inside, Wood encountered a familiar scene: "There were seven young women, I should say by appearance from 28 to 40, made up in the finest of flimsy silk dresses and then showing the daintiest of lingerie I suppose for attraction. From the passage came an entrance to a flight of stairs. Here stood Madame taking a franc for admission and I afterwards found out you paid the lady of choice any sum you cared from a franc upwards."

The French military continued operating informal brothels until the end of the twentieth century, with commanders sometimes partnering with local pimps and madams to procure sex workers for soldiers both in France and its former colonies. One state-run brothel in French Guiana continued operating until 1995.

24

Thousands of Americans Volunteered

Shortly after the First World War broke out, President Woodrow Wilson urged his countrymen to be "neutral in their hearts," but thousands of young American women and men disregarded this advice and volunteered to fight, drive ambulances, or serve as nurses in Europe—long before the US entered the war.

Most Americans joined in roundabout ways, for example claiming to be Canadian or naturalized British citizens (much easier to pull off in an era before computers and background checks). For their part, Allied recruiters desperate for new enlistees were happy not to ask too many questions. There was always the French Foreign Legion, which welcomed soldiers of any nationality, no questions asked—including about criminal convictions or fugitive status.

> "When I was asked my nationality, I drew myself up, stuck out my chest and announced boldly: 'American.' The recruiting officer calmly laid down his pen, looked at me coldly for a minute and then said in icy tones: 'Go take a walk around the block and come back here a Canadian.'"
> —*Patrick McCoy*

American volunteers favored the Allies, usually citing motivations such as friends or family connections, democratic ideals, or German atrocities like the sinking of the *Lusitania*. There were so many volunteers in France that the "American Colony" in Paris, a group representing all US expats in France, formed a special all-American ambulance division modeled on the American Ambulance, which served in France during the Franco-Prussian War of 1870–1871.

At first American ambulance drivers only served behind the front, but in early 1915 the hard-pressed French Army authorized the creation of the American Ambulance Field Service, allowing American drivers to venture into the war zone to pick up wounded directly from casualty clearing stations. Over 2,500 American drivers are credited with transporting over 500,000 wounded from French battlefields, including the inferno of Verdun.

American ambulance drivers had a distinctly literary bent. The roster included novelist Ernest Hemingway, who served in Italy and later based *A Farewell to Arms* on his experiences there; the poet and novelist John Dos Passos; the writer Gertude Stein, who drove for the Red Cross with her lover Alice B. Toklas; and noir detective genius Dashiell Hammett, author of *The Maltese Falcon* (not everyone was a writer: Walt Disney and Ray Kroc, the founder of McDonald's, trained to be drivers but never got to serve).

American volunteers also fought on—and above—the battlefields of the Western Front. In March 1916 the French Army agreed to the formation of the Lafayette Escadrille, a special squadron of American volunteer pilots (many of them drawn from the ranks of the American ambulance drivers). Originally called the Escadrille Américaine, the unit was renamed after diplomatic pressure from the US government, anxious not to violate neutrality. The Escadrille was later incorporated into the Lafayette Flying Corps of over 200 American volunteer pilots serving with French forces, including Eugene Jacques Bullard, the first African-American combat pilot, who was praised by Charles de Gaulle as a "true French hero."

At least 200 American volunteers died serving in France or Belgium before the United States entered the First World War, including 127 ambulance drivers and 49 members of the Lafayette Corps. Many were honored with the prestigious *Croix de Guerre* and *Médaille Militaire* decorations for bravery or exceptional service.   ·

25

Informal Truces Were Common

The Christmas Eve Truce of December 24–25, 1914, is one of the iconic moments of the First World War, an example of humanity triumphing over its circumstances. Across wide stretches of the front, British and German troops (and a smaller number of French and Belgian soldiers) spontaneously observed a cease-fire on Christmas Eve, leaving their trenches to fraternize with each other in "no man's land."

The official response to the Christmas Eve Truce was harsh on both sides, with severe penalties for further fraternization. But that didn't prevent similar outbreaks of brotherly love a year later, according to Henry Jones, a British subaltern, who wrote in December 1915: "We had a very jolly Christmas... In that part of the line there was a truce for a quarter of an hour on Christmas Day, and a number of Englishmen and Germans jumped out and started talking together. A German gave one of our men a Christmas tree about two feet high as a souvenir."

There were even a few strangled attempts at Christmas cheer in December 1916, although these were quickly suppressed, according to Francis Buckley, a British junior officer, who noted that a soldier

…went out into No Man's Land and had a drink with a party of them. After this a small party of the enemy approached our trenches without arms and with evidently friendly intentions. But they were warned off and not allowed to enter our trenches. This little affair, I believe, led to the soldier being court-martialled for holding intercourse with the enemy.

In fact truces weren't limited to holidays, but were fairly common on all fronts and were mostly ignored by higher-ups as long as they remained local, informal, and didn't involve actual contact with the enemy. For obvious reasons, it was easier to agree to informal truces in relatively "quiet" areas, where troops could adopt "live and let live" attitudes without blatantly disobeying orders.

In June 1915 the German soldier Adolf Benedict wrote in a letter home, censored to conceal the embarrassing truth: "We are positioned quite close to the Frenchmen and rather often we throw them over some [crossed out: sweets] and get [crossed out: chocolate] in return. The Frenchmen also throw over little pieces of paper telling us to expect a storm attack and asking us to open more intensive fire in order to prevent the attack from happening."

Of course, truces were vulnerable to the arrival of new soldiers or over-zealous officers who didn't understand (or agree to) local cease-fires with the enemy. Another German soldier, Otto Weber, later recalled a mishap during a truce:

Several times we could hear a voice from "over there" or a head appeared: "Comrade, no more bumm bumm!" Naturally, we agreed. But even if we moved more openly out of cover, the relationship towards the enemy remained still very tense anyway. One day I witnessed for example how a French post shot one of my comrades... When we protested indignantly towards the French over there, one of the Frenchmen apologized that the shooter was a very young lad and that it would not happen again.

PART 3

1915: Total War

AFTER BOTH SIDES failed to win a decisive victory in the first months of the war, they turned to inhuman new weapons and implausible new strategies in hopes of ending the stalemate. None of these gambits worked, but they managed to bring the fighting to new lows of brutality and horror.

In February 1915 the Germans, looking for ways to retaliate against the Allied naval blockade, launched the first campaign of "unrestricted U-boat warfare," giving submarine commanders permission to sink neutral as well as Allied ships without warning. However, the sinking of the passenger liner *Lusitania* with the deaths of 128 Americans in May 1915 sparked outrage in the United States, the world's most powerful neutral nation, forcing the German admiralty to call off the U-boat campaign in August.

In battle, the Germans unleashed poison gas with devastating results at the Second Battle of Ypres in April 1915, earning international condemnation even as the Allies prepared to respond in kind. In May the Germans also dispatched the first zeppelins on long-distance bombing raids against Britain, in hopes of demoralizing the civilian population (it didn't work).

For their part the Allies tried to switch things up by hitting the Central Powers in their "soft underbelly," which soon proved anything but soft. In April 1915 British and French forces mounted an amphibious assault on the Gallipoli Peninsula, guarding the approach to Constantinople, in a daring attempt to capture the Turkish straits and knock the Ottoman Empire out of the war. But the Turks had been alerted to the impending attack by the Allies' previous attempt to "force" the straits with battleships, resulting in a bloodbath when the Allied landing parties—including "Dominions" troops in the Australian and New Zealand Army Corps (ANZAC)—were forced to go ashore under heavy Turkish defensive fire. Still worse, the Allied attempt to capture Constantinople kicked Turkish paranoia into high gear, contributing to the CUP's decision to carry out a genocide against the Armenian people.

The Allies scored a major victory with Italy's entry into the war in May 1915, prompted by the mistaken belief that they were winning at Gallipoli, but the Italian front soon settled into the stalemate of trench warfare too. Then the summer and fall of 1915 brought huge setbacks for the Allies, as the Central Powers conquered Russian Poland and Lithuania in the Gorlice-Tarnow Campaign, then crushed Serbia with the help of Bulgaria (still angry about its defeat in the Second Balkan War).

On the home front the war was triggering social upheaval, as millions of women and children joined the workforce to make up the labor shortage. At the same time the unfolding disaster was also a bonanza for the United States, which not only sold weapons, vehicles, food, livestock and other supplies to the Allies, but also loaned them billions of dollars to make the purchases. US exports soared 50 percent from $2.4 billion in 1914 to $3.6 billion in 1915—and happily for American business interests, at the close of 1915 there was no end in sight.

26

Collateral Damage: The Death of Clara Haber

In the early morning hours of April 22, 1915, French colonial and Canadian troops holding the Allied line northeast of Ypres saw a strange cloud of yellow-green gas approaching across no man's land, which immediately sent thousands of terrified men streaming backward out of the trenches, blinded, coughing, choking, and vomiting, leaving at least 1,000 dead behind them.

The first chlorine gas attack of the war threatened to tear a hole in the Allied defenses, but Canadian ingenuity and bravery ultimately saved the day at the Second Battle of Ypres. Faced with a frightening new weapon, Canadian medical officers devised a simple—if disgusting—short-term defense, telling soldiers to urinate on handkerchiefs and hold these over their faces to filter the gas. The following years would see the refinement of gas masks but also deadlier gases like phosgene and mustard gas.

> "I saw one man near me turn a sickly greenish-yellow... His eyes began to bulge from his head; froth filled his mouth and hung from his lips. He began tearing at his throat. The air wouldn't go into his lungs. He fell and rolled over and over, gasping and crying out while with his nails he tore open his throat, even wrenched out his windpipe. Then his chest heaved a time or two, and he lay still."
> —*Patrick McCoy*

Fritz Haber, the German scientist who pioneered poison gas and personally supervised the use of 168 tons of chlorine at the Second Battle of Ypres, was already the savior of the German war effort—a year before war broke out.

Born in 1868, the brilliant young German-Jewish chemist (who later converted to Lutheranism) took a series of apprenticeships with chemical manufacturers serving Germany's pioneering synthetic dye industry. He then worked as a laboratory assistant at the University of Karlsruhe, where he studied electrochemistry.

Haber's research into electrochemical reduction led him to the study of nitrogen fixation, and from 1894–1911, with his assistant Robert Le Rossignol, he tackled the challenge of fixing atmospheric nitrogen in the form of ammonia at high temperature and pressure—a revolutionary process requiring large amounts of electricity (luckily Germany was a world leader in electricity production). In 1901 Haber married Clara Immerwahr, a gifted chemist who, like Haber, was a Jewish convert to Christianity, as well as the first woman to receive a PhD from the University of Breslau (now Wroclaw).

Industrialized with the help of BASF chemist Carl Bosch in 1912–1913, the "Haber-Bosch" process was rushed into service just a year later, when the war cut off Germany's access to sodium nitrate mines in Chile, the main prewar source of nitrates for gunpowder. With the German military frantically seeking new sources of nitrates for both explosives and agricultural fertilizers, BASF scaled up its production from 7,000 tons of fixed nitrogen in 1914 to 95,000 tons in 1918, or half of the Reich's total consumption (for comparison Germany's prewar nitrogen consumption was 225,000 tons, around half of it from Chile).

The synthetic production of nitrates was a critical scientific contribution to the German war effort, but it wasn't Haber's last. After the Western Front settled into stalemate in fall 1914 he proposed a radical new weapon, poison gas—not knowing one casualty would be his own wife.

The idea wasn't entirely new. Beginning in August 1914 both sides had experimented with grenades and shells containing nonlethal irritants such as tear gas. In January 1915 the Germans tried using shells containing a more lethal poison gas, xylyl bromide, at the Battle of Bolimov on the Eastern Front—but the weather was so cold the gas failed to disperse, and the attack went unnoticed.

Haber's innovations for poison gas enabled much greater scale and lethality. From his work with chemical dyes he knew that German industrial giants BASF, Hoechst, and Bayer generated huge amounts of poisonous chlorine as the byproduct of synthetic indigo—up to 40 tons a day. This could easily be weaponized, he noted, by hooking chlorine tanks up to gas diffusers on the edge of the trenches (they just had to make sure the wind was blowing in the right direction, meaning toward the enemy).

Publicly condemning her husband for committing a "perversion of the ideals of science…a sign of barbarity, corrupting the very discipline which ought to bring new insights into life," Clara Haber demanded that he stop his work on poison gas—but instead Fritz was promoted to captain and continued helping plan gas attacks on the Eastern Front. After a party celebrating his promotion, on May 2, 1915, Clara took her husband's army pistol into the garden and shot herself in the head.

Haber continued his work for the military, which he regarded as a patriotic duty, and in 1918 won the Nobel Prize in chemistry for his work on the Haber-Bosch process. This should have been the crowning achievement of a brilliant career, but after the war he was shunned by the international scientific community because of his work on poison gas. His labs also developed the pesticide Zyklon B, later used by the Nazis to kill millions of Jews (including some of his own relatives) in the Holocaust. On the other hand the Haber-Bosch process currently feeds around half the world's population, thanks to cheap chemical fertilizers.

27

Germany Encouraged the "Young Turks" to Commit Genocide

Controversy still rages over the Armenian Genocide, in which the government of the Ottoman Empire murdered around 1.5 million Armenians, most of them civilians, from 1915–1917 (the actual body count is just one area of dispute).

The modern Turkish government refuses to recognize the massacres as genocide, while apologists point to the fact that Armenian nationalists rebelled and were actively aiding Russian invaders. Historians dispute issues like the responsibility of Turkish and Kurdish civilians and whether other targeted groups, like Greek and Assyrian Christians, should also be included in the scope of the genocide.

For years controversy also surrounded Germany's support for the Young Turks' genocidal policies. German diplomats and propagandists denied the genocide was occurring and disavowed any knowledge of Turkish plans, but documents from the German foreign office archives make it clear that the Germans not only knew about the genocide—they encouraged it.

Inhabiting the Caucasus region since ancient times, the Armenians had thrived under the Ottoman Empire's governing system, which gave religious minorities the right to administer their affairs according to their own legal traditions. Armenian craftsmen, merchants, peddlers, and tinkers became the economic backbone of the region, trading with Kurdish nomads and Turkish peasant farmers.

However, the rise of Armenian nationalism in the nineteenth century undermined the system, as a new generation of Armenian thinkers, artists, and publicists demanded full autonomy or even independence. In 1890 Armenian activists founded the Armenian Revolutionary Federation, known by its Armenian acronym, "Dashnak," to fight for Armenian rights.

Armenian nationalism proved a useful tool in the hands of Russian diplomats and intelligence officers, allowing Russia to pose as the "protector" of its fellow Christians; it was no coincidence that the Dashnaks' headquarters were across the border in Tiflis (now Tbilisi), the capital of the Russian territory of Georgia. Ultimately the Russians hoped to annex Turkish territory using Armenian oppression as an excuse—and they weren't above stirring up trouble between the Armenians and their Turkish and Kurdish neighbors as a pretext.

In February 1914, under European pressure, the Turks unwillingly accepted the appointment of European administrators with sweeping legal and administrative powers to oversee seven Armenian provinces, or vilayets, in eastern Anatolia. However, they were determined to overturn the agreement and reassert control as soon as possible.

The Ottoman Empire's declaration of war on Russia in November 1914 set events in motion. After Enver Pasha's invasion of Russia ended in total defeat at Sarikamish in January 1915, the Russians pressed forward into Ottoman territory aided by Armenian rebels who served as scouts and guerrilla fighters. The Allied landings at Gallipoli on April 25, 1915, provided the final push: with the Turkish homeland threatened from east and west, the CUP ordered all Armenians—men, women, and children—"deported" to prison camps in the Syrian desert. But "deportation" really meant massacres and death marches.

Far from trying to stop them, the Germans actively encouraged their allies to settle the "Armenian question" once and for all. In December 1914 General Major Fritz Bronsart von Schellendorf, the German officer who served as Enver's chief of staff, warned that the Armenians were supporting the invading Russians and urged the Turks to take severe measures—specifically, mass deportation of the civilian population. Around the same time Lieutenant Colonel Sievert, the German officer who oversaw Turkish military intelligence, urged War Minister Enver Pasha to expand the "Special Organization," the secret police force responsible for organizing the genocide. Max Scheubner Richter, a German vice-consul who also commanded a special German-Turkish guerrilla unit, wrote of a meeting with CUP leaders:

> The first item on the agenda concerns the liquidation of the Armenians...local incidents of social unrest and acts of Armenian self-defense will deliberately be provoked and inflated and will be used as pretexts to effect the deportations. Once en route, however, the convoys will be attacked and exterminated by Kurdish and Turkish brigands, and in part by gendarmes...

German civilians not privy to the plans expressed horror at the wave of violence unleashed in the spring of 1915—not realizing their own government was complicit. The German Foreign Office promised to investigate, and CUP officials even made a show of publicly reversing some deportation measures, but these orders were secretly countermanded, and the genocide ground on. At one point Enver and his colleague Talaat Pasha demanded the recall of the German ambassador due to his Armenian sympathies, bluntly reminding Berlin "the work must be done now; after the war it will be too late."

In addition to its own horror, the Armenian Genocide set an important precedent by demonstrating that enormous crimes could be carried out with impunity, especially in wartime. Among those encouraged by the example was Adolf Hitler, who asked in August 1939 before the invasion of Poland: "Who, after all, speaks today of the annihilation of the Armenians?"

28

The Worst Job on the Zeppelin

There were a lot of unpleasant jobs during the First World War, but one of the strangest, most thrilling, and most terrifying duties of the entire conflict had to be the position of aerial observer in a German zeppelin's "spy basket."

Germany's first zeppelin bombing raids against England, beginning in January 1915, suffered from navigational difficulties due in part to Britain's notoriously bad weather, which hid towns and landmarks from zeppelin pilots and bombardiers. Simple compass navigation and dead reckoning didn't cut it, so the Germans turned to radio navigation—but this required more stable radio antennas on the zeppelins.

In April 1915 the Germans added a long line with a weight, or plumb bob, to the bottom of the zeppelins to stabilize the radio antennas. In an ingenious bit of design efficiency, they also turned the plumb bob into an aerial observation car or "sub-cloud basket" for a human observer, which could be lowered up to 3,000 feet under the zeppelin—below the cloud layer—to get a better view of the land.

This was a hazardous job in many ways, beginning with the perils of the new technology itself. Ernst Lehmann (later the captain of the ill-fated *Hindenburg*) described a bungled early attempt:

When the airship had reached a sufficient height Strasser got into the little car and gave the signal which would lower it a half mile below the ship. About 300 feet down, while the winch was allowing the cable to unwind slowly but steadily, the tail of the car became entangled with the wireless aerial. It caught the car and tilted it upside down…

Strasser…only saved himself from being tipped out by clinging to the sides of the car with a deathlike grip. Suddenly the aerial gave way, sending the car and Strasser plunging down until it brought up at the end of its own cable with a sickening jolt. It was not a propitious introduction for the new device.

The designers and crews did their best to make the spy baskets comfortable, fitting them out with wicker chairs, electric lamps, a compass, and of course a telephone to convey information to the navigators and bombardiers. However, even enclosed baskets couldn't shield the passenger from the freezing cold, frostbite, oxygen deprivation, and dizziness. In bad weather and high winds the spy baskets would rock back and forth wildly, a stomach-churning experience.

Worse still, if the zeppelin got shot down, the observer had even less time to open his parachute. This became a real possibility beginning in September 1916, when British fighter planes started using tracer bullets with incendiary magnesium that could ignite the hydrogen in the zeppelin gasbags. Not long afterward the Germans scrapped strategic bombing with zeppelins altogether in favor of raids by fast, long-distance planes, the Gotha heavy bombers.

There was one positive to the sub-cloud basket, however: unlike the rest of the zeppelin crew, who worked directly below the hydrogen-filled gasbag, the observer in the spy basket could smoke to his heart's content.

The Great Waste: Material Losses Were Insane

"You'd be surprised the amount of waste that goes on in the trenches," the poet and novelist Robert Graves wrote in his diary during the war, going on to recount this popular way to boil water for tea:

> Our machine-gun crew boil their hot water by firing off belt after belt of ammunition at no particular target, just generally spraying the German line. After several pounds' worth of ammunition has been used, the water in the guns—which are water-cooled—begins to boil. They say they make the German ration and carrying-parties behind the line pay for their early-morning cup of tea. But the real charge will be on income-tax after the war.

Indeed "total war" also meant "total waste," as mind-boggling amounts of material were destroyed in futile pursuits—or for no reason at all.

One of the most remarkable areas of waste was in artillery shells. According to one estimate, over one billion shells were fired during the course of the war—but around 15–30 percent of these were duds, due to a general policy favoring quantity over quality.

It wasn't just ammunition. While everyone was encouraged not to waste food, at the front British soldiers used unopened tins of "bully beef" as bricks to line their trench walls and army biscuits as fuel for cooking fires. Huge amounts of material were also destroyed to deny it to the enemy during retreats. But the single biggest cause of waste was the war itself, typified by artillery bombardments requiring hundreds of shells to inflict a single casualty.

"A fortune was being fired away every hour; a sum which would
send a youth for a year to college or bring up a child went into
a single large shell…an endowment for a maternity hospital was
represented in a day's belch of destruction from a single acre of
trodden wheat land."

—*Frederick Palmer*

The huge scale of spending on weapons and equipment provided plenty of cover for fraud, corruption, and war profiteering. US Treasury Secretary William McAdoo estimated that of $12.5 billion spent by the Allies in the US during the First World War, a quarter went to war profiteers. In Russia, allegations of corrupt contracts and war profiteering led to the firing of the country's first war minister, Vladimir Sukhomlinov, who was later tried on charges of treason and hindering the war effort (though only found guilty of the latter). In Britain, corruption and incompetence resulted in critical shell shortages in the first year of the war, leading to a political scandal, the "Shell Crisis," and the creation of the new office of minister of munitions, sidelining War Secretary Kitchener.

On the other hand, some waste was due to the inertia of bureaucratic procurement programs, once set in motion: the US Shipping Board spent $1.6 billion building new cargo ships *after* the armistice went into effect in November 1918.

30

Germans Sent 29 Billion Pieces of Mail During the War

In an era when telegrams were expensive and few households had telephones, regular postal service was a lifeline for soldiers at the front, allowing them to share news, receive care packages, and commiserate with friends and family—as well as transact business, pursue romantic relationships, and engage in a fair amount of idle chitchat. The only catch: everything they wrote passed under the eyes of the censors.

When the war started, the world was already in the grips of mail mania, as mass commercial printing and steam transportation enabled cheap production and distribution of postcards. In fact, the period from 1898 to 1918 is known as "the Golden Age of Postcards": in Britain alone, the number of postcards sent more than doubled from 419 million in 1904 to 900 million in 1913.

During the war tens of millions of soldiers and their loved ones turned to postcards and letters to stay in touch. The fastest, cheapest option for soldiers on all sides was the standard field postcard—a no-frills card, exempt from the usual military censorship, which could reach civilian recipients within days. However, the sender was limited to circling or underlining stock phrases such as "I am quite well," "I have been admitted into hospital," and "I have received no letter from you lately." More private communications were limited to letters, all of which had to pass the military censor.

German soldiers and civilians sent 29 billion pieces of mail over the course of the war—around 2,230 pieces of mail per soldier—including an average 7 million letters and postcards sent home by soldiers daily. On the other side, French civilians sent around 4 million letters a day to soldiers at the front and received comparable numbers back, for a total ten billion letters sent during the war. In 1917 the British Expeditionary Force handled around 2 million cards and letters per day.

> "It is extraordinary how much the mail means to people here and how many letters they write. I think getting and writing letters are the greatest relief from war. One's mind is carried away to other things. People always write apologizing for their petty doings. But these are just what we like."
> —*Oswin Creighton, Gallipoli, July 1915*

On both sides of the Western Front, letters could typically be delivered from London, Paris, Berlin, or other big cities to soldiers in the trenches within three days but took a week the other direction. Most important, bulk shipping of parcels allowed soldiers to receive care packages containing food, clothes, candy, cigarettes, and other necessities from home, and send war souvenirs as large as helmets and rifles in return. Holiday surges could be accommodated, albeit with some breakdowns: in December 1914 the French military post handled 600,000 packages per day, while British soldiers and civilians sent 4.5 million packages to and from the front in December 1916.

Regular postal service also enabled the common practice of civilians—usually women—"adopting" soldiers at the front, exchanging letters and photos of themselves as well as sending gifts and necessities. Most of these relationships with *marraines de guerre* ("war godmothers") were chaste pen pal arrangements, but there was obvious potential for romance—and with it deception. Officers censoring letters were privy to their men's efforts to "play the field": Louis Keene, a Canadian officer, recounted how one man "whom I have long suspected of being a Don Juan, had by one mail written exactly the same letter to five different girls in England, altering only the addresses and the affectionate beginnings."

Humanitarian considerations prompted both sides to enable at least limited postal service to prisoners of war, typically through neutral countries like Denmark, the Netherlands, or Switzerland. Prison mail shipments were critical for British and French POWs who faced starvation (along with the rest of the German population) due to the Allied naval blockade. By the second half of the war British and French prisoners often had better food than their captors, thanks to regular care packages from home; one French POW, Georges Connes, received over 200 packages during his three-year imprisonment, most including food.

Kraft Invents "Process Cheese"

James L. Kraft's invention of "process" (later "American") cheese during the First World War ranks among America's greatest culinary triumphs, although the guy was Canadian.

Born in 1874 on a family dairy farm in Stevensville, Ontario, in 1903 the twenty-eight-year-old Kraft emigrated to Buffalo, New York, in search of greener pastures. But his first venture ended badly, as untrustworthy partners pushed him out of his share in a dairy wholesaler. Kraft then moved to Chicago and went into business for himself, making and selling high-quality cheese from a horse-drawn wagon. After bringing his four brothers on board to help run the company in 1909, in 1914 Kraft opened his first cheese manufacturing plant, reflecting the economies of scale transforming American agriculture into big business.

From 1914–1915 Kraft conducted a number of experiments in his Chicago boardinghouse, treating and packaging cheese in order to extend its shelf life and portability without refrigeration. For his prototype cheese, Kraft melted Cheddar cheese with emulsifying salts while whisking it continuously for fifteen minutes, pasteurizing and packing the hot cheese in sterile containers.

The US Army bought 6 million pounds of the ultra-long-shelf-life cheese from Kraft for use in rations during the First World War, packaged in aluminum cans in 3- and 7-ounce sizes, which the company also marketed to consumers. In June 1916 Kraft received a patent for his "process cheese," which could be "kept indefinitely without spoiling," and launched the company's first national advertising campaigns, including most national women's magazines in 1919.

The company next introduced a cheap 5-pound brick wrapped in tin-foil, and in 1928 acquired Phenix, maker of Philadelphia Cream Cheese; by 1930, when it introduced Miracle Whip and merged with the National Dairy Products Co., Kraft supplied over 40 percent of American cheese consumption.

However, James Kraft's brother Norman, who became head of research for the company, aimed to make process cheese even more marketable by selling it pre-sliced. It wasn't until 1935 that they hit on the idea of allowing the hot cheese to spread out on a cool surface and later cut it into thin slices. Getting the product to market took fifteen more years of tinkering. 1950 brought the first "Kraft De Luxe Process Slices," followed in 1965 by the first individually wrapped singles. Today American cheese is typically a mix of Colby and mild Cheddar.

32

Kids at War

"My best sniper turned out, when his parents at last traced him, to be only fourteen years old," recalled Lieutenant Stuart Cloete of the 9th King's Own Yorkshire Light Infantry. "He was the finest shot and the best little soldier I had. A very nice boy, always happy. I got him a military medal and when he went back to Blighty and, I suppose, to school, he had a credit of six Germans hit."

It's hard to know exactly how many children (defined as individuals under the age of eighteen) served in the First World War around the world, but the number was probably in the millions. Britain alone allowed a quarter of a million underage boys to enroll in the military, as British and Dominion recruiters conveniently forgot to ask for birth certificates; the youngest casualty at Gallipoli, the Australian soldier Jim Martin, died of typhoid at the age of fourteen. The Royal Navy had long admitted cadets and boy seamen as young as twelve; Jack Cornwall, a sixteen-year-old gunner, met a hero's death during the Battle of Jutland.

It was also common to see children serving on the Eastern Front, especially in Cossack units, where service sometimes began in the preteen years. Violetta Thurstan, a British nurse volunteering with the Russian Army on the Eastern Front, noted in early 1915:

There was one small Cossack boy who was riding out with his father to the front and who could not have been more than eleven or twelve years old. There are quite a number of young boys at the front who make themselves very useful in taking messages, carrying ammunition, and so on. We had one little boy of thirteen in the hospital at Warsaw, who was badly wounded while carrying a message to the colonel, and he was afterwards awarded the St. George's Cross.

There were instances of even younger children serving. The youngest soldier known to have served in the war was the Serbian Momčilo Gavrić, who was seven years old when he joined the Serbian Army after Austro-Hungarian troops killed his entire family. Gavrić, who survived the war and passed away in 1993 at the age of eighty-six, was one of the lucky ones. As the Serbian Army retreated through Albania in the fall and winter of 1915–1916, the government ordered around 30,000 Serbian boys ages twelve to eighteen to accompany the army into exile—a death sentence for most, as around 23,000 died of starvation and exposure in the mountain winter.

Fortunately, most children didn't have to fight in the war, but many participated in other ways. In Britain, Boy Scouts helped the war effort by guarding telegraph towers, bridges, and railroad tracks against saboteurs, and also helped during air raids by giving the all-clear. British Girl Guides maintained hostels and first aid stations, tended gardens to ease food shortages, and helped charities package clothes and other donations for men at the front.

Most importantly, vast numbers of children joined the industrial workforce to help ease labor shortages. In 1917, British Education Minister H.A.L. Fisher estimated that there were 600,000 children under the age of twelve working in British war industries and agriculture, while in France 133,000 children made up 10 percent of the munitions labor force. In Germany shortages forced the government to transfer 1 million students from schools to farm work, and across all the combatant nations children were forced into backbreaking agricultural labor along with women.

33

Russian Jews Were Glad to See the Germans

During the Second World War, Eastern European Jews living in Poland and the Soviet Union were terrified by the arrival of Nazi German invaders accompanied by *Einsatzgruppen,* or "special action groups"—mobile death squads who murdered around 1.5 million Jews in mass shootings and "gas vans" from 1939–1943. This experience couldn't be more different from the First World War, when Russian Jews greeted the Germans as liberators.

Russia had long been notorious for rabid anti-Semitism, encouraged by the tsarist regime to distract attention from its own shortcomings. Russian peasants blamed Jews for all manner of fictitious crimes. The tsarist secret police stoked the hatred by publishing the fabricated *Protocols of the Elders of Zion* in 1903. In the nineteenth and early twentieth century anti-Semitic hatred boiled over in a series of pogroms or mob violence against Jews across Russia, Ukraine, Belarus, and Russian Poland, killing thousands and driving thousands more to emigrate.

The First World War only served to heighten anti-Semitism in Russia, as the tsarist regime feared the Russian Jews would collaborate with the Germans in revenge for the pogroms. In the "Statute of Administration of Troops in Wartime" issued on July 29, 1914, the Russian high command authorized the mass deportation of up to 1 million Jews from Russia and occupied territories into exile as far away as Siberia, while Russian soldiers murdered, raped, and abused Jews who remained. Helena Jablonska, a Polish woman living in Russian-occupied Galicia, described the round-up of Jews in her diary on April 17, 1915:

The Jewish pogrom has been under way since yesterday evening. The Cossacks waited until the Jews set off to the synagogue for their prayers before setting upon them with whips. They were deaf to any pleas for mercy, regardless of age... Some of the older, weaker ones who couldn't keep up were whipped... They say this round-up is to continue until they've caught all of them. There is such lamenting and despair! Some Jews are hiding in cellars, but they'll get to them there too.

Although few places matched the ferocity of popular anti-Semitism in Russia, "polite" anti-Semitism remained common around the world, with anti-Semitic activists pushing for more sinister measures. Germany was no exception: in 1916, at the urging of anti-Semitic politicians, the German Army carried out a "Jewish census"—only to find, much to its embarrassment, that Jews were actually overrepresented in its ranks.

34

Gunther Plüschow:
The Only POW to Escape Britain

The First World War featured plenty of high adventure, but few could match the epic wartime career of Gunther Plüschow.

Born in Munich, Bavaria, in 1886, when war broke out the dashing twenty-eight-year-old Plüschow was the only German Navy pilot on active service in Tsingtao, China. He took part in the defense of the German colony during the siege by Japanese and British forces from August 27 to November 7, 1914, carrying out aerial reconnaissance of Allied ships and troop movements and harassing the enemy with bombs improvised from coffee tins.

When Tsingtao finally fell before waves of Japanese infantry, Plüschow managed to escape in his plane to southern China, where he was forced to ditch in a rice paddy, later setting fire to his plane. With the help of an American missionary, Plüschow made contact with local Chinese officials who put him aboard a junk to Nanking. There the Chinese decided to intern Plüschow, as required by neutrality rules, but he dodged his guard and escaped to Shanghai by train.

Presenting himself as a wealthy Englishman, Plüschow bought passage to the United States on an American mail ship, the *Mongolia*, which departed Shanghai on December 5, 1914. Plüschow stayed aboard ship as it docked at three Japanese ports, feigning illness with the help of a friendly doctor and pulling his quilt up over his face when customs inspectors came calling, then endured a two-day typhoon before arriving in Honolulu.

In Hawaii Plüschow's true identity was finally revealed, but the intrepid fugitive kept moving, boarding another ship for San Francisco, where he received a celebrity reception on December 30, 1914, and partied away New Year's Eve with new American friends in one of the city's best night clubs. On January 2, 1915, he boarded a cross-country train with a handful of German expatriates who were also hoping to return home, stopping to see the Grand Canyon and Chicago before arriving in New York City, where he noted pro-Allied sentiments but blamed it on English propaganda.

Assuming a new identity as a Swiss locksmith, Plüschow bought a berth in steerage aboard the Italian steamer *Duca Degli Abruzzi*, bound for Naples, and almost made it to still-neutral Italy, from which he could have reached safety in Austria-Hungary. But during a stop in Gibraltar on February 8, 1915, a shipboard spy pointed Plüschow out to British authorities, who became even more suspicious after finding money and a revolver hidden in his clothes. Plüschow was arrested and transported to England, where he disclosed his true identity and was imprisoned in a prisoner-of-war camp in Dorchester before being transferred to a prison camp for officers at Donington Hall in Maidenhead, Derbyshire.

After five months in captivity Plüschow decided to escape from the island. On July 4, 1915, during a thunderstorm Plüschow and a fellow prisoner fluent in English, Trefftz, hid in a small cave on the castle property until nightfall, with fellow POWs covering for them at roll call and lights out. After carefully crossing several barbed wire entanglements and fences with the help of wooden planks, Plüschow recalled:

Cautiously we went forward in the darkness, crossing a stream, climbing over a wall, jumping into a deep ditch, and at last slunk past the guard-house which stood at the entrance to the camp. Only after that were we in the open. We ran without stopping along the wide main road which led to Donington Castle... We now opened our bundles, took out civilian grey mackintoshes, and walked down the road in high spirits as if we were coming from a late entertainment.

Disguised as working-class Englishmen, from Derby they bought train tickets first to Leicester then London, which Plüschow had visited as a tourist just two years before. The pair split up, and Trefftz was soon apprehended, but Plüschow eluded authorities by sleeping in gardens and parks near other vagrants. Hoping to board a neutral ship without identification papers or passport, in July 1915 Plüschow switched disguise again, donning a dirty blue suit and darkening his hair with Vaseline and coal dust to impersonate a ship hand; he ate in local workingmen's pubs, paying with a small fund of shillings contributed by the other POWs in Donington Hall.

Plüschow made several failed attempts to swim out to Dutch steamers lying at anchor in the frigid Thames, while spending his days in London parks and movie and music halls. Following a number of failed attempts to steal a rowboat, Plüschow finally succeeded in commandeering an unguarded dinghy, which he rode downstream and concealed onshore.

After another day hiding out, he rode the tide upstream to a Dutch steamer, the *Princess Juliana*; jumped on a mooring buoy; and climbed the anchor chain to the main deck. Waiting until the sentries were distracted flirting with stewardesses, Plüschow lowered himself to the cargo deck and hid in a lifeboat covered by a canvas tarpaulin. He endured the elements during the slow North Sea crossing, then casually disembarked in Flushing, Netherlands, pretending to be a crewmember as he helped moor the ship. Staying the night in a hostel, he finally boarded a train for Germany the next day, where he was arrested as a spy before his real identity was confirmed.

Plüschow's incredible feats won him the Iron Cross First Class, enduring fame in Germany, and grudging respect in the Allied nations.

35

Flying the Friendly Skies

In a conflict defined by hate and misery, there seemed to be one shining exception: the war in the air, where dashing pilots mounted their modern warhorses and rode forth for glorious single combat. Of course, this vision was sanitized, romanticized, and distorted (by the end of the war single combats were rare, with most dogfights involving multiple planes). But in some regards it was accurate, as many pilots embraced chivalrous ideals, treating their foes with elaborate courtesy when they weren't actively trying to kill them. A German pilot, Hans Oluf Esser, described a collegial encounter with a vanquished French foe in July 1916:

> I fly round him several times, waving my handkerchief, and he also shows a white flag. I then make a beautiful landing beside him, just in time to stop him setting fire to his machine. He came up to me and said in German, "You are surely no N.C.O.?" and then he introduced himself, "Lieutenant Jean Raby." I did the same, and we shook hands... In the afternoon we were both invited to coffee with the Flight, and smoked the pipe of peace.

The etiquette of the aviation brotherhood extended to long-running correspondence between enemy air squadrons, dropped from planes, sometimes with gifts (real or gags). Bernard Pares, a British observer with the Russian Army, noted the exchange of letters with Austrian flyers as well as a flamboyant gift in April 1915: "On Easter Sunday an enormous Easter egg, with the inscription in Russian 'Christ is risen,' was dropped from an aeroplane and, having a parachute attached to it, fell slowly on the Austrian lines."

In summer 1917 a British medical officer, Oskar Teichman, noted that his section of the Egyptian Expeditionary Force received messages from a German pilot culminating in a tongue-in-cheek farewell in June 1917: "In the morning Fritz dropped a note offering to fight any five of our aeroplanes, and later on he dropped another message saying good-bye, and adding that he had come down to the Palestine front for a rest cure and was now returning to France."

36

Some Guys Have All the Trucks

Mass-produced motor vehicles played a defining role in the First World War. Together with rail networks and old-fashioned horsepower (still the backbone of local transportation) they allowed the rapid movement of men, ammunition, and supplies to the war zone. The British Expeditionary Force traveled to battlefields across the Western Front aboard a fleet of London double-decker buses, and the "Miracle on the Marne" of September 1914 was made possible by the Paris "taxi lift" of soldiers to reinforce the French Sixth Army.

The western Allies, Britain and France, enjoyed a sizeable lead over Germany in motor vehicles, reflecting their prewar advantage in automobile production as well as their ability to tap American industry, by far the world's largest exporter of motor vehicles.

From 6,000 trucks and automobiles in 1914, the French Army's vehicle fleet grew to around 80,000 in 1918; one of the most noteworthy achievements of the war was the French "*camion*" service's continual convoy of 3,500 trucks on the only road into Verdun (later dubbed "The Sacred Way"), supplying the French defenders with food and ammunition during the German siege in 1916. Over the same period the number of vehicles of all kinds possessed by the British Expeditionary Force increased from a few hundred in 1914 to 122,000 by the end of the war, including 56,000 trucks, 23,000 cars, and 34,000 motorcycles.

Trucks played a central role in the logistics network that kept the French and British Armies supplied with ammunition, food, and other necessities. Henry Jones, a young British supply officer, described the vehicles required to supply just one division in his diary in June 1916:

"Our column numbers no fewer than 150 lorries, 6 motor-cars, and 20 motor-bikes, and about 600 personnel, not to speak of a big travelling workshop and two or three break-down lorries."

> "The vehicles in the long processions that were winding their way on every road were numbered by the thousands and as far as one could see in every direction there was a seething mass of men and vehicles and horses, broken here and there by great piles of the materials of war. It was like a gigantic ant heap. At first we received the impression of great disorder and confusion, but on closer observation we saw that every man had his place and every movement its purpose."
> —*Paul Cravath, on British preparations for the Somme, June 1916*

On the other side, from 3,500 trucks available across all of Germany in 1914, the German Army's truck fleet grew to around 30,000 vehicles by the end of the war, with production increasing to around 12,000 per year. The Germans faced a number of obstacles to production: most importantly, parts weren't standardized, reflecting the small, artisanal German prewar automobile industry. When war broke out the German Army was forced to offer a special subsidy to truck makers who met army specifications.

Germany was also cut off from rubber supplies in Brazil, prompting the army to equip many trucks with steel-rimmed wheels (a jolting experience for passengers). Meanwhile Germany's ally Austria-Hungary had fewer than 20,000 automobiles in service in 1916, and never produced more than 2,000 trucks per year.

37

US Supplied Most of the Allies' Oil

America not only supplied huge numbers of cars and trucks to the Allies—it was also the source of most of the diesel fuel and gasoline that powered them.

While the US was one of the world's leading importers of oil for most of the second half of the twentieth century, during the first half of the century it was actually the world's largest oil exporter, mostly thanks to Texas. In 1914 the US pumped 266 million barrels of oil, or 65 percent of the world's total production, rising to 413 million barrels, or 71 percent of the total, by 1918.

Most of this went to domestic consumption, but the US also managed to supply 80 percent of the wartime oil demands of the western Allies. In 1918 alone America exported 559 million gallons of gasoline and 1.2 billion gallons of fuel oil. When the final Allied drive unfolded on the Western Front from July to November 1918, thousands of tanks and motorized infantry units were powered by American fuel.

On the other side, the Central Powers relied almost entirely on oil production in the Austrian province of Galicia, which was occupied by the Russians from 1914–1915, raising the prospect of an energy crisis. The tables turned in summer 1915 when the Central Powers recovered the Galician oil fields, followed a year later by the conquest of Romania, Europe's largest oil producer. In one of the dramatic episodes of the war, British engineers under Colonel Jack Norton-Griffiths mounted a desperate last-minute attempt to wreck the Romanian oil fields in Ploiești, north of Bucharest, destroying hundreds of wells, storage tanks, and refineries and burning around 800,000 tons of oil. However, German engineers lived up to their reputation for efficiency, repairing the fields and raising production to 2.7 million barrels in 1917 and 8.7 million in 1918, ensuring the Central Powers had adequate supplies for the rest of the war.

Meanwhile the war also saw the beginning of America's creation of an international oil empire, as big US oil companies elbowed into foreign markets to take over production, refining, and distribution. The first big target was Mexico, where US investments in the oil industry jumped from $85 million in 1914 to $200 million by 1919. Over the course of the war US imports of oil from Mexico more than doubled to 41 million barrels by 1918 (most of it re-exported after refining).

The Mexican venture came to an unhappy end in 1938, when the Mexican government announced a sweeping nationalization of all the country's petroleum resources and infrastructure following labor disputes with foreign oil companies (March 18, "Oil Expropriation Day," is still a national holiday in Mexico).

Canary Girls

With tens of millions of men called away to war across Europe, maintaining production of ammunition and critical war goods required drafting millions of women into the labor force—a revolution in gender relations, as young women gained economic and personal independence with factory jobs. In all the combatant nations, women's participation in the war effort also justified demands for greater political power, eventually winning women the right to vote in Europe and America.

However, war work could also be incredibly dangerous, especially for the women and girls who filled each shell of high explosives by hand. In addition to all the normal boredom and aches and pains of assembly line work, they faced the constant danger of explosions, which could be triggered by mere static electricity, as well as the risk of amputation by machinery working with shell casings. On a weirder note, many women turned yellow, prompting the nickname "canary girls."

> "Nearly every baby was born yellow. Mum said you just took
> it for granted it happened and that was it. You were tougher in
> those days than what they are today!"
> —*Gladys Sangster*

The yellow-orange color was caused by regular contact with large amounts of trinitrotoluene (TNT) powder. Their hair turned blond on top, in contrast to their natural color by their roots, adding to their unusual appearance. One worker, Ethel Dean, recalled: "Everything that that powder touches goes yellow. All the girls' faces were yellow, all round their mouths. They had their own canteen, in which everything was yellow that they touched… Everything they touched went yellow—chairs, tables, everything."

Unfortunately, the yellow hue wasn't the only side effect of working with TNT: doctors reported 400 cases of toxic jaundice among factory workers during the war, 100 of which proved fatal. The canary girls also complained of nausea, skin irritation and hives, respiratory illnesses, and digestive issues. Even more troubling, pregnant canary girls often gave birth to yellow babies; however, the yellow color gradually faded, and the canary babies don't appear to have suffered long-term side effects.

39

The Allies Violated Neutrality Too

Britain entered the First World War because of Germany's invasion of neutral Belgium in August 1914, with much talk of the "rights of small nations." But during the war the Allies didn't hesitate to violate the neutrality of weak countries. Greece is a pretty good example.

The Allies first tried to persuade the Greeks to join them with the successful Italian strategy of propaganda, bribery, and territorial promises and enjoyed an advantage thanks to pro-Allied Prime Minister Eleutherios Venizelos. But there was also a major obstacle in the form of Greece's King Constantine, who was married to a German princess. In March 1915 Constantine dismissed Venizelos for offering to help the Allies without consulting the rest of the government, but the elder statesman remained influential and soon returned to office.

With Greek politics deadlocked, the Allies resorted to the much simpler approach of issuing demands at gunpoint. As the Central Powers prepared to invade Serbia in fall 1915, the British and French urgently needed to send reinforcements to help the Serbs, but the only route was through the northern Greek port of Salonika. The Allies sent 150,000 troops to occupy the city at the "invitation" of Venizelos, who once again requested Allied "assistance" without getting permission from Constantine or Parliament. At the last minute they caved, since it was now pointless to resist. The reinforcements arrived too late to help Serbia, but the British and French went on to occupy a large portion of northern Greece for the rest of the war.

The Allies were still determined to get the Greeks into the war, whether they liked it or not. After ratcheting up the pressure with an economic blockade, in spring 1916 they staged a coup in Salonika, installing Venizelos as the leader of a new parallel government, which immediately declared war on the Central Powers. Seizing control of the Greek telephone and telegraph system in October 1916, the Allies demanded the Athens government hand over the Greek Navy; when Constantine rejected the Allied ultimatum, they occupied Athens and tightened the economic blockade.

With starvation threatening southern Greece and the Allies in charge in all but name, in June 1917 Constantine abdicated and went into exile in Switzerland, allowing his pro-Allied son Prince Alexander to take the throne. Venizelos returned to Athens in triumph aboard a French ship and formed a new government, which immediately declared war on the Central Powers, giving Greece the distinction of declaring war twice.

The Ku Klux Klan Was (Re)Founded During the War

After the South's defeat in the Civil War, in 1866 former Confederate soldiers founded the first Ku Klux Klan as a secret fraternal organization, supposedly intended to protect Southern civilians against rapacious Union soldiers and resist Reconstruction. The Klan's founders elected former rebel cavalry commander Nathan Bedford Forrest as its "Grand Dragon" in 1867.

Along with other groups like the Red Shirts and the White League, the KKK terrorized freedmen to prevent them from asserting their legal rights or organizing politically. But in 1869 Forrest, apparently believing it had gone too far, ordered the organization to disband. Meanwhile, Congress passed the Force Acts, allowing President Grant to deploy federal troops to fight the Klan and other white paramilitaries across the South, marking the end of the first KKK. After a disputed presidential election in 1876, Southern Democrats let Republican Rutherford B. Hayes take the White House in return for withdrawing federal troops from the South, ending Reconstruction (and selling out the freedmen) in what became known as the "corrupt bargain." By 1900 most Southern states had passed "Jim Crow" laws to disenfranchise African Americans, reestablishing white supremacy across the former Confederacy, buttressed by an informal reign of terror known as "lynch law."

However, the First World War threatened to disrupt Southern society once again, as hundreds of thousands of African Americans headed north for well-paid factory jobs making munitions and other war goods in northern cities. The "Great Migration" threatened to undermine the

Southern economy by removing its main source of cheap labor, and Southern whites also feared blacks would become more assertive, since they now had other options on the table. At the same time, growing numbers of Catholic and Jewish immigrants unnerved white Protestants across America.

> "This was in the early autumn of 1915. The World War was on, and the Negroes were getting pretty uppity in the South about then. The North was sending down for them to take good jobs. Lots of Southerners were feeling worried about conditions."
> —*William Joseph Simmons*

These mounting tensions gave birth to the second incarnation of the KKK as a racist, anti-Semitic, and anti-Catholic hate group. Inspired by the glowing depiction of the first KKK in *Birth of a Nation*, D.W. Griffith's inflammatory silent film epic, on November 25, 1915— Thanksgiving Eve—a salesman from Alabama named William Joseph Simmons announced the "rebirth" of the KKK with a cross burning ceremony attended by fifteen followers on Stone Mountain, Georgia. Simmons anointed himself "Imperial Wizard of the Invisible Empire of the Knights of the Ku Klux Klan, Incorporated."

As the name indicates, the KKK was an open secret: *The Atlanta Constitution* ran a breathless item describing the Stone Mountain ritual, and Simmons registered the group with Georgia as a corporation. In fact, the KKK was a multilevel marketing scheme as much as anything else. By 1921 Simmons had recruited around 100,000 followers and netted $1.5 million selling officially licensed Klan robes and paraphernalia. The group soon built a factory to supply growing demand and began investing in real estate in Atlanta, including the construction of an "Imperial Palace" for

Simmons costing $45,000, a huge sum. By 1923 the KKK was bringing in $12 million per year.

The KKK's virulent rhetoric and acts of violence were widely condemned, but the organization also wielded growing political power, so the police mostly left it alone (and in many places were sympathetic, if not actual members themselves). It found even more new recruits outside the former Confederacy, as the Great Migration and an influx of European war refugees brought growing tensions to Northern cities in the late 1910s and 1920s, sparking a series of race riots in cities and towns including East St. Louis, Philadelphia, Washington, DC, Chicago, Omaha, and Tulsa.

By 1925 the KKK claimed 4 million members across the US, over 3 percent of the country's population. While this was probably an exaggeration, that year it staged a march in Washington attended by 50,000 members, testimony to its wide reach and political power, followed by another impressive rally in 1926. However, the passage of severe restrictions on immigration in 1924, along with the adoption of informal segregation in Northern cities (through practices like real estate covenants and the redrawing of school districts), removed much of the original impetus for the group, which saw its membership decline sharply to around 30,000 by 1930. It remained dormant until the organization of the third KKK in the 1960s to oppose the African-American civil rights movement in the South.

41

Henry Ford's Peace Ship

In 1915 Henry Ford organized a bizarre expedition to Europe in hopes of somehow brokering peace on the war-torn continent, leading to the saga of the Peace Ship (widely mocked as the "Ship of Fools"). Like many Americans, Ford believed the war was a senseless waste and publicly urged an immediate end to the bloodshed. His heartfelt condemnations attracted the attention of American journalist Louis Lochner and Hungarian pacifist Rosika Schwimmer, who claimed to have secret letters showing that the combatants were ready for peace.

The documents later turned out to be fakes, but Ford became convinced he could use his fame and fortune to help end the war in Europe. In 1915, he chartered an ocean liner, the *Oscar II*, and invited hundreds of pacifists, politicians, religious leaders, and intellectuals on a voyage to Europe, where they would use the publicity surrounding the mission to shame the opposing sides into sitting down for peace talks.

It didn't turn out quite like they'd hoped. The first setback came before the ship even set sail, with US president Woodrow Wilson's refusal to officially endorse the mission. In addition, the press was painting Ford as a crackpot.

Pressing on, the Peace Ship left Hoboken, New Jersey, but once at sea the peace delegates soon fell to arguing over what response they should make to Wilson's call for increased US military spending. The ship made it as far as Oslo in neutral Norway, but Ford and a number of other passengers caught the flu, forcing the industrial magnate to return home to recuperate.

Nonetheless the Peace Ship sailed bravely onward for over a year, until early 1917, when America's looming entry into the war made the already absurd project pointless, and Ford pulled his funding.

PART 4

1916: The Long Haul

AFTER A YEAR and a half of war, it was clear to everyone that the conflict had spiraled beyond the control of any government and was likely to continue for years. As ordinary soldiers and civilians on both sides settled in for the long haul, the generals desperately looked for ways to end the stalemate, while political leaders nervously noted growing anger on the home front over catastrophic casualties and growing shortages of food, fuel, and other necessities.

In 1916 both sides mounted their biggest offensives on the Western Front so far: the German assault on the key French fortress of Verdun, and the simultaneous British and French attempt to break through the German defenses on the Somme. The battles of Verdun and the Somme were breathtakingly bloody—July 1, 1916, the first day of the Somme, cost the British 57,470 casualties, including 19,240 dead—but failed to deliver the hoped-for strategic victories.

By the summer of 1916 things looked grim for the Central Powers. In June Russia launched its most successful campaign of the war, the Brusilov Offensive, forcing the Germans to call off Verdun so they could prop up their embattled ally Austria-Hungary. In August the Italians scored a surprise victory at the Sixth Battle of the Isonzo, and the Romanians—thinking the Allies were near victory—declared war on Austria-Hungary. The Allies had more good news in the Middle East, where in June 1916 the Sharif of Mecca, Hussein bin Ali, launched the Arab Revolt against Turkish rule with promises of help from the Allies. In October 1916 his son, Prince Faisal, would meet a British intelligence officer, T.E. Lawrence, who would help lead the Arab Army to victory.

The Allied winning streak wasn't going to last. The First World War was characterized by sudden, surprising shifts in the fortunes of all the combatants, and by the end of the year the Central Powers were on the upswing again. In October 1916, the Central Powers unleashed a devastating counterattack on the Romanians, storming the mountain passes of the Southern Carpathians in winter conditions and conquering the capital, Bucharest, by December. On the Western Front the Allied offensive on the Somme had failed decisively by November 1916, and the French Army was exhausted after Verdun.

Across Europe ordinary people were suffering more than ever. The German potato harvest failed due to potato blight, resulting in starvation in Germany during the winter of 1916–1917. The period was remembered as the "Turnip Winter," with a death toll including 80,000 children (by the end of the war around 750,000 Germans would die from starvation and malnutrition). In Russia, the tsarist regime faced wave after wave of strikes, including several in which police refused to fire on protesters.

Calculated Carnage: Verdun

More than any other battle, Verdun came to symbolize the mindless waste of the First World War. Perhaps most horrifying is the fact that the German general who planned the campaign never really wanted to capture the town in the first place.

The geographic gateway to France from Germany's Moselle region, Verdun was surrounded by a ring of modern concrete and steel forts built on both banks of the Meuse River beginning in the 1890s. Along with Toul, Épinal, and Belfort, it formed a wall of fortifications on the French frontier with Germany, and the German decision to attack through Belgium in 1914 was prompted by the need to avoid the fortresses. Their reputation deterred German attacks until February 1916, when chief of the general staff Erich von Falkenhayn put his cynical plan in motion.

> "Within our reach behind the French sector of the Western front
> there are objectives for the retention of which the French General Staff
> would be compelled to throw in every man they have. If they do so the
> forces of France will bleed to death—as there can be no question of a
> voluntary withdrawal—whether we reach our goal or not."
> —*Falkenhayn, December 1915*

Falkenhayn planned an all-out attack on Verdun, called Operation "Gericht" or "Judgment"—but never really intended to capture the town. Instead, he coldly (but correctly) calculated that the French would commit every last resource to saving Verdun, now a symbol of French resistance to the foreign invaders. The Germans just had to get close enough to threaten Verdun, then dig into strong defensive positions and massacre the French as they counterattacked. Falkenhayn intended to defeat France through attrition, tricking the French into flinging tens of thousands of men to their deaths in wave after wave of futile infantry attacks.

There were a couple of problems with this ruthless plan. Ever secretive, Falkenhayn apparently hid his true intentions from the German Crown Prince Wilhelm, who as commander of the German Fifth Army would be responsible for implementing Operation Gericht and believed he was really supposed to capture the citadel. Additionally, Falkenhayn failed to realize that an objective with symbolic importance for the enemy might acquire similar meaning for Germans—and failure to capture it would have political consequences.

The Battle of Verdun soon took on a deadly life of its own. After the bloody opening assault on February 21–28, 1916, German officers in the field—unaware of the attrition plan and hoping for a breakthrough— kept advancing rather than digging in at strong defensive positions, as Falkenhayn had anticipated. German casualties ended up being almost as high as the French, spelling the failure of Falkenhayn's attrition plan, and with it his job as chief of the general staff. In September 1916, he was given a field command and replaced by General Paul von Hindenburg.

43

Casualties at Verdun and the Somme Equaled the Entire US Civil War

A few amazing numbers can help convey the incredible scale of bloodshed in the First World War. One of the most remarkable: the death toll of two battles on the Western Front in 1916, Verdun and the Somme, was equal to all four years of the US Civil War.

To be fair these battles were like wars themselves. The Battle of Verdun, which lasted from February 21 to December 18, 1916, was a cynical ploy by German chief of the general staff Erich von Falkenhayn to bleed the French Army white. Meanwhile 150 miles to the west, the Battle of the Somme from July 1 to November 18, 1916, saw the British and French mount a gigantic attempt to break through German lines—only to become bogged down in rain and mud. Both battles fell short of their aims, causing far more casualties than the attackers expected.

> "We all carried the smell of dead bodies with us. The bread we ate, the stagnant water we drank… Everything we touched smelled of decomposition due to the fact that the earth surrounding us was packed with dead bodies."
> —*German soldier at Verdun*

Over the course of ten bloody months French and German forces suffered around 1 million casualties at Verdun, including approximately 162,000 French dead and 143,000 German dead. Meanwhile at the Somme both sides suffered a total of over 1.3 million casualties, including 127,000 British dead—Australian, New Zealand, Indian, South African, and Canadian troops among them—along with 164,000 Germans and 51,000 French; like Verdun, the near-equal figures for total dead indicate that the Allied strategy at the Somme was also a failure.

Adding up the dead from both battles, Verdun and the Somme claimed the lives of around 647,000 people. For comparison, over four years from 1861–1865, the American Civil War claimed the lives of 618,222 men who died fighting for the Union or Confederacy, as well as from disease, starvation, and exposure (although some historians place the death toll as high as 750,000).

Half the Easter Rising Leaders Were Poets

Ireland is a legendarily literary nation, so it's fitting that half the leaders of the failed Easter Rising of 1916 were poets, and most of the rest were journalists or essayists. The literary bent was no coincidence, as Irish nationalism was intertwined with a cultural revival focused on the Gaelic language, especially poetry and literature.

Ireland had risen up against the English a number of times in its history, but before the First World War it looked like self-government was finally within reach. After years of controversy, on May 25, 1914, the House of Commons passed the Third Irish Home Rule Act, which would allow Ireland to rule itself. But the Protestant population of Ulster County in Northern Ireland, fearing oppression by the island's Catholic majority, bitterly opposed home rule. Both sides had formed paramilitaries for "self-defense," with the Protestant, pro-British Ulster Volunteer Force facing off against the nationalist, mostly Catholic Irish Volunteers.

Things became even more complicated when Protestant officers in the British Army refused to act against their co-religionists in Northern Ireland, an incident known as the Curragh Mutiny after the base where they were stationed. On July 21, 1914, King George V called the opposing sides together for a "peace conference" at Buckingham Palace, but the dispute was put on the back burner after Austria-Hungary's ultimatum to Serbia on July 23.

The situation reached the boiling point in September 1915, after the cabinet suspended Irish home rule as an emergency measure until the war was over. The radical wing of the Irish Volunteers—most of them members of the secret Irish Republican Brotherhood (IRB)—began plotting to win independence by force. On April 24, 1916, Easter Monday, around 1,250 rebels in Dublin rose up against British rule in hopes of inspiring a broader rebellion across Ireland, which failed to materialize; afterwards the execution of sixteen leaders by the British contributed to the revolutionary mood in Ireland, setting the stage for the Irish War of Independence and Irish Civil War from 1919–1922.

The leaders in 1916 were short on military experience but long on literary talent. Patrick Pearse, the commander in chief of the Irish rebels who read out the Proclamation of the Republic from the steps of the General Post Office, was a poet and writer as well as headmaster at St. Enda's, a secondary school for boys. Joseph Plunkett, who helped organize German support for the rebellion, was a poet, journalist, and the founder of the *Irish Review*, a literary and political journal. Another leader, Thomas MacDonagh, was a poet and editor of the *Irish Review* and also helped found the Irish Theatre, a patriotic dramatic organization.

Journalists formed another key part in the leadership, reflecting their importance as propagandists. Thomas Clarke, the first signatory of the Proclamation of the Republic, had been a journalist and editor of *The Gaelic American*, an Irish nationalist newspaper based in New York City.

Most of the other Irish leaders had artistic talents or interests. Éamonn Ceannt was a talented musician who once performed for the Pope. James Connolly, a Scottish-born union leader, had advocated the adoption of Esperanto, the new world language invented by L.L. Zamenhof, a Polish ophthalmologist. Others at least dabbled in poetry and literature: Éamon de Valera, the American-born future taoiseach (prime minister) and president of Ireland, wrote the poem "Invocation to the Sacred Heart" before receiving a last-minute reprieve from execution in 1916, perhaps due to his US citizenship.

Lord Kitchener Was Killed
by a British Ruse Gone Wrong

The death of British Secretary of War Horatio Herbert Kitchener at sea, five days after the bloody but inconclusive Battle of Jutland, was a blow to the British public.

On the morning of June 5, 1916, Kitchener boarded a British destroyer in Thurso, Scotland, which took him across the Pentland Firth to the huge British naval base at Scapa Flow. Here he boarded a fast, armored cruiser, the HMS *Hampshire*, bound for Russia via the northern route through the Barents Sea to the northern Russian port of Archangel.

Kitchener was supposedly going to Russia to discuss the war situation with Tsar Nicholas II, but he also looked forward to the trip as a sort of working vacation, accompanied as always be his aide-de-camp (some said gay lover) Colonel A.O. Fitzgerald. For their part Kitchener's colleagues in the cabinet welcomed it as a chance to get the old man out of the way for a few weeks. Some speculate that Kitchener was also escorting a very large sum in gold bricks to the embattled Romanovs.

After having lunch with Admiral John Jellicoe aboard his flagship, the *Iron Duke,* Kitchener boarded the *Hampshire* and weighed anchor for Russia at 4:45 p.m. in the middle of a gale. At Jellicoe's order, instead of heading directly into the North Sea, the *Hampshire* first sailed into the Pentland Firth and took a longer, more sheltered route north, hugging the west coast of the Orkney Islands, where it could move faster to better evade enemy submarines. After several hours the *Hampshire*'s captain, Herbert Savill, ordered two destroyer escorts to head back because of the heavy seas.

Between 7:30 and 7:45 p.m. on June 5, 1916, the *Hampshire* was rocked by a huge blast and immediately began taking on water. The ship had hit a German mine, and the lifeboats were of limited use because of the storm and rough water; within fifteen minutes the *Hampshire* sank with the loss of at least 643 men, including Lord Kitchener, leaving just twelve survivors.

Unsurprisingly Kitchener's death sparked an outpouring of grief and anger, including predictable conspiracy theories blaming British turncoats, communists, and Irish nationalists, among others.

In fact, there was clear evidence of negligence. British naval intelligence had intercepted three communications from Germany to the mine-laying submarine *U-75*, determined to be operating off the western Orkneys at this time, its presence subsequently confirmed by sightings. For some reason, the Admiralty failed to heed these reports, along with three additional warnings from naval intelligence on the day Kitchener sailed.

As it happened, *U-75* was in the area because of an elaborate but ultimately unsuccessful attempt at deception by naval intelligence. Before the Battle of Jutland, Director of Naval Intelligence Admiral Hall had staged a fake transmission, supposedly from a British destroyer, indicating that a particular channel off the west Orkneys had been cleared of mines on May 26. Hall apparently hoped that the Germans would intercept the message and send U-boats to re-mine the route (which was actually rarely used) before the battle—perhaps in hopes they could be trapped and destroyed.

As it happened a dozen German submarines were deployed around Scotland and the Orkneys before and during the Battle of Jutland, including *U-75*, which laid twenty-two mines in the waters off the west Orkneys again on May 28, including the mine credited with sinking the *Hampshire*. Due to excessive secrecy and the distraction of the Battle of Jutland, Hall's naval spies failed to alert Jellicoe to the British gambit before he ordered the *Hampshire* to take the alternative route because of the storm.

46

Avalanches Killed 50,000 on the Italian Front

Soldiers on both sides of the mountainous Italian Front faced some of the most extreme conditions of the war. Trenches had to be blasted out of solid rock with dynamite or built with stones and cement under enemy fire, while explosions produced clouds of tiny slivers of rock, at least as dangerous as shrapnel.

In the highest elevations, simply getting soldiers and supplies up to the front required feats of engineering. In addition to tiny railways, tunnels, and switchback roads carved out of mountainsides, the Italians and Austrians built networks of steam-powered "funiculars" and aerial trams or *telefericos*, resembling modern-day ski lifts, with cables stretched between pylons and pulleys. Closer to the front complex systems of "ropeways" and ladders allowed the soldiers to reach precarious frontline positions.

> "The Italian campaign in the mountains is the greatest
> engineering job ever undertaken by man."
> —*Will Irwin*

No surprise, mountain warfare claimed a heavy toll through accidents and disasters, including thousands of troops who froze or fell to their deaths. Over the course of the war avalanches killed 50,000 soldiers on both sides of the Italian Front, including 10,000 Austrian and Italian soldiers who perished in the Tyrol region during just a few days in mid-December 1916. In one incident on December 13, approximately 200,000 tons of snow and rock killed 300 Austrian troops on Mount Marmolada, though another 200 were rescued. The accidents prompted one Austrian officer to observe, "The mountains in winter are more dangerous than the Italians."

47

Get the Guest

Soldiers received meager rations and were usually forced to spend their own money during rest periods in "billets," when they were quartered with peasant families who were the only game in town for eggs, milk, butter, meat, bread, and vegetables (not to mention alcohol) and gladly used their monopoly position to squeeze their uninvited guests. Less scrupulous soldiers—meaning most of them—returned the favor by stealing food from peasants every chance they had.

Some troops were especially easy marks: Canadian, Australian, and American troops all received high pay compared to their French and British comrades and had a reputation for extravagant spending, making them even more attractive targets. Where a British Tommy didn't make much more than a shilling or 15 cents and French *poilus* received 5 *sous* or around 8 cents per day, Australians got 6 shillings per day, Canadian privates were paid $1.10 Canadian, at that time on par with the US dollar, and American privates received $1 US (although all were encouraged to send their pay home for families and to buy war bonds).

The phenomenon of locals ripping off hapless dupes from out of town wasn't limited to Europe. In America, a soldier from New York State suspected northern recruits were being cheated during a train stop in rural Virginia: "The train is standing in the Salisbury depot, where I have bought an apple-pie. Everyone seems to know the Seventh [Division] by reputation, and charge us accordingly. It is a crime."

Souvenirs and Talismans

By most accounts life in the trenches alternated between short bursts of terror and long stretches of boredom, so frontline troops found various ways to keep themselves occupied, including crafting and DIY projects. This "trench art" typically used materials readily available in their immediate surroundings, such as cartridge and shell casings, empty grenade cases, and shrapnel.

One of the most common forms of trench art was decorated shell casings, which soldiers etched, hammered and embossed, and preserved as souvenirs, sometimes commemorating particular battles or places where their unit served. Some of these designs incorporated inlaid copper or silver, and artists with metalworking skill could turn shell casings into usable objects such as beer steins, pitchers, or tobacco jars.

Another popular kind of trench art was jewelry, including rings, bracelets, necklaces, and brooches made from the nose cones and brass fittings of dud shells, which soldiers wore themselves or sent home for wives and girlfriends. Once again these could serve a commemorative purpose and incorporated additional decorative items like buttons from captured enemy uniforms. By contrast other creations were strictly utilitarian, such as watch chains or lighters improvised from cartridge casings.

No surprise, DIY pastimes were also popular in prisoner-of-war camps (at least, among officer POWs who weren't employed in war-related industries). Georges Connes, a French POW held at a German fortress in Mainz, wrote in his diary:

The painters paint, the sculptors sculpt, the engravers engrave, the bookbinders bind books... For the individuals who have patience but no creativity there is *kerbschnitt*, which consists of carving with special wood ornaments based on ready-made models; there is also tarso, which consists of painting and varnishing them in a way that imitates inlaid work... There is no shortage of those who enjoy netting (embroidery) and tapestry.

In addition to crafting, soldiers everywhere were keen collectors, as reflected in the universal hunt for trophies like enemy helmets, bayonets, badges, and medals (not to mention more gruesome souvenirs such as enemy skulls). On a more mystical plane, millions of soldiers carried special objects or charms to ward off enemy fire. E.M. Roberts, a British pilot, noted that "each man had his own little fetish. It was known as the pocket-piece or mascot. In some cases, it might be a dice or a playing-card... In other cases, it might be a locket, then again a medal, while many of us carried little woolen dolls. Even photographs were said to have the quality which we expected of our fetishes."

Germans Used Cargo Subs to Evade the Allied Blockade

With British and French ships sweeping the seas of German merchant vessels, the Germans soon hit on an obvious solution: just go under them. The result was two cargo submarines that evaded the Allied naval blockade to transport high-value exports to the United States and bring back scarce, crucial war supplies.

In 1916 the North German Lloyd Line built two giant cargo submarines, the *Deutschland* and *Bremen*, both over 300 feet long with a cargo capacity of over 700 tons. Because of their limited cargo space, the Germans sensibly focused on shipping low-volume, high-priority goods. On the first trip to the US in June 1916, the *Deutschland* carried chemical dyes, pharmaceutical products, gems, and mail, altogether worth $1.5 million, or around $34 million today. When the sub arrived in Norfolk and Baltimore on July 9, 1916, it caused a sensation in the American press.

"Norfolk Amazed By Deutschland. Merchantman Submarine's Siren Tells of Wonderful Craft's Arrival. Escapes Warships Close To Coast. Took No Chances And Submerged When Smoke Was Seen, Says Captain."
—New-York Tribune, *July 10, 1916*

On August 2 it departed on its return trip carrying 341 tons of nickel, 93 tons of tin, and 348 tons of crude rubber (with typical ingenuity, 257 tons of rubber were transported in the extra space between the pressure hull and outer hull) with a total value of $17.5 million or $396 million today. The *Deutschland* made a second round trip to New London, Connecticut, in November 1916, carrying gems and medicines and returning with 6.5 tons of silver, among other high-value goods.

Due to the relatively short lifespan of electric batteries needed for submerged propulsion, the submarines made most of the journey on the surface using diesel engines, only submerging in the blockade zone or when nearing unknown vessels. However, the journey to the US was still hazardous: leaving New London on its second return trip the *Deutschland* accidentally collided with a local tugboat, which sank with the loss of five crewmembers. The *Bremen* was lost at sea in mysterious circumstances sometimes in late 1916 or early 1917 while en route to Norfolk, Virginia.

The Germans ultimately built seven submarines in the large U-151 class, including the *Deutschland* and *Bremen*, but after the US entered the war in 1917, the Imperial German Navy requisitioned all of them and armed them for combat service. The *Deutschland* had a successful second career as a long-distance U-boat, sinking forty-two ships with a combined total tonnage over 120,000 tons by the end of the war.

Central Powers Unleashed a Wave of Sabotage Across the US

During the period of US neutrality the Central Powers were cut off from American resources by the Allied naval blockade, while the French and British were free to tap America's vast production, key to maintaining the Allied war effort. Unable to buy American goods themselves, German and Austro-Hungarian spymasters were determined to at least slow American war production for the Allies by stirring up unrest among workers and industrial sabotage. Toward that end the German ambassador to the US, Johann von Bernstorff, received a pile of cash and secret instructions: "Avail yourself in unlimited amounts of these credits for the destruction of the enemy's factories, plants and...setting incendiary fires to stocks of raw materials and finished products."

The results included some very, very large fires and explosions. One of the first big industrial plants to be targeted was a factory in Trenton, New Jersey, which mass-produced "structural wire" used in submarine nets and artillery chains. On the night of January 18, 1915, unknown saboteurs cut the wires for the fire safety system and set fire to piles of cotton waste, destroying an eight-acre site including the factory and workers' houses. Happily, none of the 300 employees was killed.

This and other brazen acts of sabotage outraged American public opinion after US intelligence agents seized secret documents containing details of the covert Central Powers campaign, published by the *New York World* in August 1915. In September 1915 the US government angrily demanded that Austria-Hungary recall its ambassador, Baron Konstantin Dumba, after he admitted organizing attempts to sabotage munitions production, followed by the German diplomats Franz von Papen and Karl Boy-Ed in December 1915.

But the sabotage continued. On November 10, 1915, Bethlehem Steel's largest artillery shop was totally destroyed by a mysterious fire; the next day arsonists destroyed another factory in Trenton, New Jersey. In February 1916 a grand jury in San Francisco indicted the German consul, Franz Bopp, and thirty-one others on charges of conspiracy to sabotage munitions factories (bizarrely Bopp would later become a silent film star, while Papen became the last German chancellor before Hitler). In April 1916, German agents were charged with conspiring to sabotage industrial canals and bomb cargo ships.

By far the biggest bang occurred on July 30, 1916, at 2:08 a.m., when a stupendous explosion leveled Black Tom Island, a cargo facility in Jersey City, New Jersey, connected to the mainland by a causeway and railroad bridge. Under cover of darkness German saboteurs set a number of fires on a pier where a barge carrying 100,000 pounds of high explosives bound for Russia was moored. This explosion in turn triggered around a thousand tons of explosives in neighboring warehouses. Remarkably the Black Tom Island explosion killed only four people but injured hundreds more and shattered windows as far away as Times Square in Manhattan.

51

140,000 Chinese Laborers Worked on the Western Front

During the Great War ordinary people around the world suddenly found themselves swept up in the maelstrom, including countless civilians who performed backbreaking manual labor as part of work battalions.

Among the millions who found themselves suddenly transported to a strange land was the Chinese Labour Corps, consisting of around 100,000 Chinese workers recruited by the British Army to perform manual labor on the Western Front, along with another 40,000 Chinese workers recruited by the French.

The British recruited the first contingent of Chinese laborers to deal with a looming manpower shortage in May 1916. Pay was relatively generous, with a signing bonus of 20 yuan and a salary of 10 yuan a month, and most of the recruits were peasants, accustomed to physically taxing work including unloading cargo ships, digging trenches and graves, and building roads. More skilled laborers were employed as mechanics and craftsmen. Overall, around 10,000 Chinese workers died during the war from wounds, accidents, and disease—especially the flu.

The Chinese made up about half the total foreign labor force in France and the Middle East, which also included 100,000 Egyptians, 21,000 Indians, and 20,000 black South Africans. After the war, almost all were repatriated.

52

Science Marches On: Einstein's General Theory of Relativity

The biggest war in history couldn't stop one of its biggest scientific discoveries—Albert Einstein's revolutionary theory of relativity, which changed our understanding of the laws of nature forever.

Before Einstein, scientists viewed the world through the lens of physical laws formulated by the great British scientist Isaac Newton in the seventeenth century. These mathematical rules explained things like gravity, the movement of planets, and the behavior of light in an orderly, predictable way. According to Newton's "universal law of gravitation," all physical phenomena occur in a uniform way, regardless of the position or movement of the observer. But as time went on some troublesome inconsistencies emerged: for example Newtonian physics' failure to explain the unusual orbit of Mercury around the sun, which revolves over time, creating a "daisy petal" pattern.

In the first years of the twentieth century the German scientist Albert Einstein realized that Newton's concept of a uniform universe wasn't accurate. Drawing on the work of contemporaries and his own unique insight, Einstein used a series of "thought experiments" to show that physical phenomena actually look different to observers in different places depending on their own state of motion. In other words, space and time are not fixed but changeable, even if we don't notice it in our daily lives.

In 1905 Einstein presented his "special theory of relativity," which suggested that matter and energy are interchangeable; this prompted his former teacher, Hermann Minkowski, to theorize that space and time are fundamentally linked in a four-dimensional "space-time continuum." In

1907 Einstein predicted that gravity would "bend" light far more than Newton allowed, although he underestimated how much at first. Continued work yielded his theory of static gravitational fields in 1912, predicting that time would slow down near large objects with strong gravity. As a corollary of this theory Einstein also predicted that dying stars would collapse in on themselves, sometimes forming black holes—hugely powerful gravity wells capable of sucking in light and stopping time. Importantly, he also suggested a way to test his prediction that gravity could bend light, by observing light from distant stars around the sun during an eclipse (during ordinary conditions the sun's own light would make it impossible).

From 1912–1914 Einstein began formulating his "general theory of relativity" with the help of his friend Marcel Grossmann, an expert in advanced mathematics—not Einstein's strong suit—showing that space-time and gravity were linked by the mathematics of curvature. In August 1914, he looked forward to testing the theory's predictions with the help of astronomers observing a solar eclipse over the Crimean Peninsula—but the war made these observations impossible.

Now competing with the great British mathematician David Hilbert to prove his own theory, Einstein became uneasy about some of its shortcomings, including its failure to fully explain the unusual orbit of Mercury. In November 1915, he began a frantic series of revisions, sending breathless updates to the Prussian Academy of Sciences, each correcting the previous one, at the rate of one per week. On November 25, he finally presented the general theory of relativity to the academy in Berlin, including the crucial "field equations of gravitation," explaining Mercury's orbit. He published a version with further refinements in a German science journal, *Annalen der Physik,* in March 1916.

53

Life Was Tough in Neutral Countries

For most people, the First World War summons images of soldiers suffering in the trenches, while civilians endured anxiety and hardships at home. But it also made life hard for the citizens of neutral nations, who had to deal with economic and social disruption, refugees, food shortages, and epidemics.

Some of the hardest hit were the small nations caught—literally—between the combatants in Europe: Switzerland, the Netherlands, Denmark, Sweden, and Norway. Bending over backward to maintain their neutrality, they still faced extortionate demands from the opposing sides, which then hypocritically accused them of aiding the enemy.

Before the war all the European neutrals depended on food imports from their bigger neighbors and other parts of the world, but shortages in the Central Powers and the Allied naval blockade cut off most of these sources (the Allies stopped shipments to the neutrals, too, arguing they might resell them to the enemy). In response neutral governments instituted rationing, "meatless days," anti-hoarding rules, and bans on alcohol, as well as stopping exports of their own precious grain and livestock. After obtaining strict promises not to re-export food, the Allies eventually eased up on the blockade a bit, but wartime inflation and unemployment meant many people still went hungry: by July 1918 over one-fifth of the population in Basel, Switzerland, relied on daily visits to soup kitchens to survive.

Meanwhile the combatant nations weren't shy about shaking the neutrals down whenever they felt like it, using the threat of starvation or invasion. In spring 1918 the Netherlands and Sweden both agreed to give up part of their merchant fleets to the Allies in return for food. That summer Germany, facing starvation itself, "borrowed" livestock from the Netherlands with a thinly veiled threat to take them by force.

Despite these hardships the neutrals played a major humanitarian role by accepting huge numbers of refugees. In 1914 the Netherlands alone accepted over 1 million Belgian refugees who stayed for the duration of the war, making food shortages even worse. The neutral nations also agreed to intern prisoners of war from both sides who were too sick or badly injured to fight: from 1916 and 1918, Switzerland accepted 68,000 French, German, and British soldiers, saving many POWs from starvation. Sir Evelyn Grant Duff, the British ambassador to Switzerland, recalled their arrival: "Our men were simply astounded. Many of them were crying like children, a few fainted from emotion. As one private said to me: 'God bless you, sir, it's like dropping right into 'eaven from 'ell.'"

With borders open to both sides, neutral nations also became hotbeds of espionage. Switzerland was particularly popular among spooks and revolutionaries. Lenin met with the German intelligence agent "Parvus" in Switzerland in May 1915, and issued his first call for world revolution at a socialist conference there a few months later. In 1917 Lenin snuck back into Russia via Sweden, another neutral.

Last but not least, neutrals helped end the war by providing safe harbor for the losers. On abdicating in November 1918 Kaiser Wilhelm II fled into exile in the Netherlands as a guest of his distant cousin Queen Wilhelmina, who in 1920 refused the Allies' demand to extradite him for prosecution for war crimes. Wilhelm remained in the Netherlands until his death in 1941, during the Nazi occupation in the Second World War (the Nazis had little use for the ex-kaiser, blaming him for Germany's previous defeat).

America's Tobacco Conquered the World (Especially China)

The Americas were the birthplace of tobacco, and in the nineteenth century Americans pioneered the production of mass-produced cigarettes. But most foreign markets remained dominated by British companies until the First World War, when American rivals took advantage of the global disruption to muscle them aside.

The turn of the century had seen fierce international competition between British and American tobacco companies, with the latter playing offense. In 1884 James Buchanan Duke of North Carolina licensed inventor James Bonsack's machine for automatically rolling cigarettes, drastically lowering the price and creating a mass market dominated by Duke's company, American Tobacco (Duke used robber baron tactics, like selling below the cost of production, to drive competitors out of business).

At first cigarettes were considered low-class compared to cigars and pipes, due to their association with poor European immigrants, but their popularity among soldiers in the Spanish-American War gave them greater respectability and made American Tobacco one of the biggest companies in the world.

After several years of bruising competition, in 1902 American Tobacco and the British Imperial Tobacco Company joined forces to form a trust, the British American Tobacco Company, with both sides agreeing not to compete with each other on their home turf and split the sales in new markets. American Tobacco dominated the BAT, holding twelve out of eighteen seats on the board of directors and two-thirds of the stock.

The BAT trust continued until 1911, when the US Supreme Court broke up American Tobacco under antitrust laws. The American partner was also forced to sell its stake in BAT, putting the firms in competition once again. But like Standard Oil, American Tobacco's successor companies—American Tobacco, R.J. Reynolds, Liggett & Myers, and Lorillard—still cooperated, wielding enormous collective power.

The First World War upended the world tobacco market to America's advantage, as British companies lost access to sources of Turkish tobacco in the Ottoman Empire and Balkans and faced shipping disruptions. At the same time war fueled demand for pre-rolled cigarettes, which were easier for soldiers to carry and smoke than loose tobacco.

The most dramatic shift occurred in the vast Chinese market, long the jewel of the British international tobacco business. China was already a massive consumer of cigarettes, mostly thanks to BAT executive James Thomas, an American who'd pioneered mass-produced printed advertisements blanketing the country and offered salesmen (most of them Americans fresh out of college) $500 bonuses for learning Chinese in the prewar period.

During the war, the Americans reconquered the Chinese market at the expense of their former British partners. The American invasion was led by a new company, Tobacco Products Corp. (later part of Philip Morris), formed with backing from James B. Duke as a holding company to manage tobacco exports in competition with BAT.

However, the cigarette honeymoon in China didn't last: after the war ended BAT revived its trade, and during the Second World War most foreign tobacco companies in China were seized by the Japanese.

55

Plastic Surgery Was Developed During the War

Plastic surgery has been around for thousands of years: sometime between 1000 and 600 B.C.E. the ancient Indian doctor Sushruta described techniques for reconstructing ears and noses, repairing cleft lips, and performing skin grafts. However, plastic surgery became the subject of intensive scientific study during the First World War, when dozens of new techniques were developed to treat mutilated soldiers (although in some cases these were adaptations of ancient ideas).

The First World War left 23 million men wounded, often receiving multiple injuries over the course of the conflict, and at least 8 million veterans were permanently disabled. It's hard to know how many suffered mutilating facial wounds, but a few numbers convey the scale of the problem: during the Battle of the Somme in 1916, over 2,000 British soldiers received facial injuries requiring surgery, and in 1917 the Queen's Hospital in Britain devoted 1,000 beds solely to the treatment of facial injuries. Over 300,000 soldiers in the German Army received head injuries during the war.

Even more than the loss of limbs, mutilating facial injuries presented a huge obstacle to veterans returning to ordinary civilian life—but it wasn't totally hopeless, thanks to recent advances in medical science. While Alexander Fleming's discovery of penicillin didn't come until ten years after the war, during the nineteenth century the British surgeon Joseph Lister pioneered sterile surgery, and dentists and surgeons figured out how to use ether, opiates, and other sedatives for general anesthesia.

In the war surgeons on both sides made major advances in reconstructive surgery. Harold Gillies, a New Zealand–born surgeon serving in the

Royal Army Medical Corps, pioneered techniques including repurposing tissue from other parts of the body to make new facial features. In one remarkable example, Gillies—inspired by an ancient technique described by Sushruta—was able to build a new nose by transplanting cartilage from the rib cage under the skin in the patient's forehead. After new blood vessels grew and the skin healed, in a second operation the cartilage and skin were twisted down over the patient's face and formed into a new nose. This was then allowed to heal before a third surgery removed excess tissue from the brow area—leaving the patient with only minor facial scars.

"After I finished my duties I went up into one of the wards to see an English soldier who is having practically a whole new face made. His nose, upper jaw, and upper face were shot away… He now has a nose and upper face, and said that next week he was going to have another operation, and have an upper jaw and lips made. He spoke about it as you would of having a new suit made."
—*Mary Smith Churchill*

Gillies's greatest innovation was his discovery of a way to perform skin grafts from virtually any part of the body with a very high success rate. Previously skin grafts had often failed because the tissue died after it became separated from its blood supply or exposed to infection. Gillies figured out how to migrate skin grafts by forming the tissue into a "tube pedicule," which remained attached at one end of the body, maintaining its blood supply, while the other end was attached to the transplant site—essentially "walking" the grafts over the patient's body to the area where it was needed.

Of course, some injuries were too severe to be repaired, leaving the wounded men with the choice of wearing masks and enduring public scrutiny or becoming shut-ins. In France, the *gueules cassées* ("smashed faces") wore partial or complete masks to conceal their injuries. In Britain, the government designated special park benches for men with severe facial injuries, painted blue to alert other visitors that they might see upsetting injuries.

On a more positive note the war saw numerous other medical advances in addition to plastic surgery, including blood transfusions and the creation of the first "blood banks," with "citrated" blood stored ahead of time available by the Battle of Cambrai in November 1917. Where stored blood was unavailable, blood transfusions were performed "live," from a healthy individual to the person experiencing blood loss (the most important thing was making sure the donor didn't have syphilis). There were also major advances in surgical techniques for serious injuries: from 1916 to 1918 the survival rate for combined chest and abdominal surgeries rose from 18 percent to 67 percent.

However, there was wide variation in medical expertise and available facilities across the war zone, and wounded soldiers on other fronts were often condemned to very primitive treatments. Lady Kennard, volunteering as a nurse on the Romanian front, described a terrible scene during the Central Powers invasion in late 1916: "In our English hospital there is a man who has had his foot amputated. He lay pinned under a burning car. A hatchet was brought by a doctor to a French officer standing near, and the doctor said: 'Do it if you can; I have no instruments and feel paralysed.' The Frenchman did the thing in the whole horror of the sunlight…"

56

Animals Received Medals Too

The First World War was a human tragedy, but animals played key roles in the war effort on all sides as well, suffering, dying, and performing remarkable feats of bravery and endurance. Some were even decorated for their valor.

Besides horses the most commonly used animals were dogs: the German Army employed around 30,000 dogs over the course of the war, the French 20,000, and the Italians 3,000, along with tens of thousands more on other fronts. Dogs were trained to perform sentry duty; join infantry attacks (the "dogs of war"); pull machine guns, supply wagons, or sleds; and deliver messages on the battlefield, as well as food, water, and cigarettes. During the Battle of Verdun a black border collie-greyhound mix, Satan, saved the lives of a French fortress garrison by delivering a crucial message along with two carrier pigeons in cages strapped to his sides so they could respond; Satan's handler was killed by a German sharpshooter while shouting encouragement to the dog, who was shot twice in the legs and died of his wounds after completing the mission.

Search and rescue dogs saved thousands of lives by locating badly wounded men in the battlefield (or avalanche victims on the mountainous Italian front). Another French dog, Prusco, was credited with saving over 100 wounded men in a single day, dragging some to safety himself, but most dogs worked with human handlers. Malcolm Grow, an American surgeon volunteering with the Russian Army, described a rescue dog in action on the Eastern Front:

A rocket shot up, and over the parapet a yard to my right I saw a shaggy head peering down. The dog held something in his mouth. I heard him whine softly... In the light of my electric torch I saw that he held in his mouth a crumpled, blood-stained cap. His master took the cap in his hand, snapped the leash on the dog's collar, lifted him up on the parapet and crawled up after him, followed by two stretcher-bearers. The dog led them out through the barbed wire, tugging at his leash…

A number of dogs were decorated for their service in the war. Sergeant Stubby, a brindle terrier mutt rescued from the streets of New Haven, Connecticut, in 1917, became the mascot of the American 26th Division in France, and proved his worth in battle by warning of poison gas attacks, locating wounded American soldiers, and supposedly even capturing a German soldier who surrendered to the dog. Stubby earned one wound stripe and three service stripes, was promoted to sergeant, and in 1921 received a special gold medal from former American Expeditionary Force commander John "Black Jack" Pershing. Sergeant Stubby and his adoptive soldier, Robert Conroy, later earned a small fortune in theatrical appearances, leading parades, and other civic functions.

Amazing feats were also performed by homing pigeons, which could carry important messages long distances when other communications were severed; in recognition of their importance, the first British "Defense of the Realm Act" made it a crime to kill, wound, or imprison a pigeon. In October 1918 one British homing pigeon, Cher Ami, helped save the lives of 194 American soldiers from friendly fire by carrying a message telling their artillery to stop firing. After two other pigeons were shot down by the Germans, Cher Ami survived a gunshot wound to her breast and leg and the loss of an eye to fly 25 miles to her headquarters in less than half an hour. Cher Ami's heroic service in this and previous battles—she also served in Verdun—earned her the French Croix de Guerre with Oak Leaf Cluster. US Army medics crafted her a tiny new wooden leg, and after the war Pershing personally organized her transport to the US in a private berth. After dying of her wounds in 1919, Cher Ami was preserved by taxidermists and is now on display in the Smithsonian.

Other animals also served in the war, sometimes in surprising ways. Dogs, cats, birds, and slugs were used to provide early warning against poison gas, and British soldiers carried jars of glowworms to read maps at night when their flashlight batteries ran out. However, not every idea worked out: a British attempt to train seagulls to blind U-boats by relieving themselves on the periscopes came to nothing.

Finally, animals of all kinds served as mascots or simply as pets, comforting and entertaining troops. American volunteer pilots in the Lafayette Escadrille somehow obtained two lion cubs, Whiskey and Soda, as their mascots, causing some consternation when they visited Paris on leave. A Canadian officer brought a black bear named Winnipeg to England, who was sensibly allowed to stay at the London Zoo and later became the inspiration for Winnie the Pooh.

57

Lawrence of Arabia Kind of Hated Camels

Another animal, the camel, played a key role in the war in the Middle East, used by both Allies and Turks for transportation during their desert campaigns. The biggest camel-enabled success story was the Arab Revolt, in which small groups of Bedouin warriors led by Prince Faisal and his adviser, the British intelligence officer T.E. Lawrence, rode camels to strike isolated Turkish outposts and dynamite railroads across the Hejaz in what is now western Saudi Arabia, culminating in the conquest of Damascus, Syria, in 1918.

Camels were obviously indispensable for the campaigns carried out by Faisal's forces. Able to survive over a week without water and several months without food, the hardy animals were perfectly adapted to the Arabian Desert, where small natural wells were located up to 100 miles apart, and grazing was usually limited to gnarled scrub and seasonal grasses. But that didn't mean they were pleasant to ride or be around.

In fact, Lawrence confessed that, at least sometimes, "I hated the beasts, for too much food made their breath stink; and they rumblingly belched up a new mouthful from their stomachs each time they had chewed and swallowed the last, till a green slaver flooded out between their loose lips over their side teeth, and dripped down their sagging chins."

Of course, it's worth noting that according to Lawrence's own account, he also hated animals in general, if only for metaphysical reasons: "…I would always rather walk than ride for hatred of animals… For me there was something disagreeable and hurtful to my pride in the sight of these lower forms of life. Their mere existence seemed a servile reflection upon our human kind, the sense with which a god would look on us…"

To be fair, he wasn't a big fan of people either, holding himself to an impossible moral ideal and looking down on anyone else who didn't: "To put my hand on a living thing was defilement; and it made me tremble if they touched me or took too quick an interest in me. This was an atomic repulsion… [I] lamented myself most when I saw a soldier with a girl, or a man fondling a dog, because my wish was to be as superficial…"

The upside of his bizarre outlook was that Lawrence looked on physical suffering as a test of character, allowing him to perform remarkable feats and inspire his men to do the same. However, the story that he crossed the impenetrable Nefud Desert to attack the key Red Sea port of Aqaba, as depicted in the classic film epic *Lawrence of Arabia*, is false; they actually took a relatively safe, roundabout route that avoided the desert.

58

Everyone Hated Each Other— Especially Their Own Allies

Just because people found themselves fighting on the same side didn't mean they liked each other—quite the opposite. In fact, the saying "familiarity breeds contempt" might have been coined for the First World War, when being shoved together by circumstances seemed to bring out the worst on all sides.

Defeat in battle was the main source of tension, as reflected in the famous exclamation often attributed to Erich Ludendorff, Germany's top strategist, when asked about Germany's hapless ally Austria-Hungary: "Ally? We are shackled to a corpse!" The overbearing Germans in turn were thoroughly disliked by their Turkish allies, according to Lewis Einstein, an American diplomat in Constantinople, who noted that Turkish officers complained they were being used as cannon fodder: "There are more reports of growing ill-feeling between Turks and Germans. The former complain that they are sent to attack while the Germans remain in safe places…"

Tension also arose from the fact that German and Austrian officers received better food, lodging, and medical care than their Turkish comrades. The Spanish consul in Jerusalem, Conde de Ballobar, noted in November 1916:

Truly the contrast is notable in this Austrian-German-Turkish entente. The Teutons and Austrians live the life of princes: Sanatoriums, hospitals magnificently equipped, automobiles, economical restaurants, great free warehouses, very well stocked, while the Turks do not even have shoes, eat almost nothing and are lodged and cared for any old way.

On the other side, the Entente Cordiale and wartime cooperation couldn't erase the historic rivalry between Britain and France dating back centuries. Ordinary French and British people often butted heads over social and cultural differences, as well as the inevitable disputes between soldiers and civilians. The poet and novelist Robert Graves remembered:

On the whole, troops serving in the Pas de Calais loathed the French and found it difficult to sympathize with their misfortunes… I wrote home about this time: "I find it very difficult to like the French here, except the occasional members of the official class… I have not met a single case of the hospitality that one meets among the peasants of other countries. It is worse than inhospitality here, for after all we are fighting for their dirty little lives."

There was also a kaleidoscopic array of prejudices and dislikes within the British Empire, including the Dominions of Canada, South Africa, Australia, and New Zealand. ANZAC and Canadian troops alleged that British officers were indifferent to their heavy casualties at battles like Gallipoli, the Somme, Vimy Ridge, and Passchendaele. For their part, the British were often shocked by the lack of discipline and rambunctious behavior of some Dominion troops. A British aristocrat volunteering in the British medical corps, Private Robert Lord Crawford, complained in his diary in April 1916:

The Australians do small credit to our army or their continent. They drink a great deal too much and are followed about by crowds of open mouthed French children—one sees men brandishing empty bottles, making speeches, reeling about, and in general behaving in a foul and disgraceful manner… Our men, even those whom we qualify as boozers, are frankly ashamed of our compatriots. The French are disgusted.

THE ANGLO-SAXONS

How the English Became the English?

PART 5

1917: Breaking Points

THE FOURTH YEAR of the war started and ended with upheaval. During the first Russian Revolution of March 1917, angry workers and soldiers in Petrograd overthrew the incompetent Tsar Nicholas II and his wife Alexandra. Russia's liberal parliamentarians established a new Provisional Government, which continued fighting alongside Britain and France, but it was forced to share power with the socialist Petrograd Soviet, foreshadowing trouble in the near future.

Also in March 1917, the Germans staged a surprise withdrawal from the area around the Somme to the Siegfried Line—a 70-mile-long stretch of concrete fortifications in the center part of the Western Front known to the Allies as the "Hindenburg Line." The withdrawal eliminated two salients around the Somme, shortening the length of the Western Front and detaching thirteen German divisions for service in other theatres.

After this strategic victory came Germany's worst strategic mistakes. The resumption of unrestricted U-boat warfare on February 1, 1917, followed by public confirmation of the outrageous Zimmermann Telegram in March, brought what may be considered the decisive event of the war: on April 6, 1917, the United States declared war on Germany, ultimately spelling doom for the Central Powers. However, in the short term the US remained all but powerless, with a prewar military numbering around 180,000 men (in comparison, in 1916 Germany had 8.2 million men under arms). The American war effort would begin with a gargantuan program of conscription, construction, and training, ultimately creating an army of around 4 million by the end of 1918.

The US entered the war in the nick of time: following the failure of the Nivelle Offensive on the Western Front in April 1917, in May the French Army was racked by mutinies, apparently inspired by the Russian Revolution, threatening to paralyze the Allies. To pick up the slack the British launched another giant offensive at the Third Battle of Ypres, better known as Passchendaele, resulting in around half a million casualties on both sides, followed by another push at the Battle of Cambrai, where they experimented with a sneak attack led by tanks.

After an optimistic outlook for the Allies in the first half of 1917, the end of the year saw their fortunes plunge (again): in October Germany and Austria-Hungary unleashed a crushing offensive against Italy at Caporetto, occupying a large part of northern Italy by the end of December and forcing the British and French to hurry reinforcements to prop up the Italians. Then in November Lenin's Bolsheviks overthrew Russia's weak Provisional Government, effectively taking Russia out of the war, freeing up 1 million German troops for a knockout blow against the Allies on the Western Front in spring 1918. Their salvation depended on one question: would the Americans arrive in time?

59

Allies Painted "Dazzle Ships" Weird Colors and Patterns

The First World War saw pioneering advances in the art of camouflage, which aimed to conceal—or simply confuse. While most camouflage on land was meant to hide objects like guns and dugout entrances from observation by scouts or aerial reconnaissance, at sea it had a rather different purpose: causing eyestrain.

Realizing that no amount of paint could make ships disappear, given other clues like wakes and smoke from their funnels, British camouflage artists working for the Admiralty decided to take a different approach. Rather than hide the ships, they would simply make it more difficult for enemy observers to judge their distance, speed, and direction of travel.

The result was the "Dazzle ships," which bore what might be called the opposite of camouflage: insanely eye-catching, wildly patterned paint jobs combining shapes and colors to confuse the eyes of enemy U-boat commanders watching the ships through periscopes. Dazzle ships used a number of visual tricks to distort perspective: seemingly parallel lines actually tapered toward each other to make it look as if the ship was headed in a different direction, while intersecting candy stripes and grids of brightly colored squares appeared blurry at a distance. False bow waves made the ships look like they were traveling faster than they really were, and three-dimensional images playing off the ship's contours further confounded depth perception.

60

The US Let Germany Use Its Telegraph (and Guess What Happened)

After Britain declared war on August 4, 1914, it immediately used its overwhelming naval power to cut Germany off from the outside world. As a naval blockade stopped foreign trade, on August 5 the British General Post Office cable ship *Alert* embarked on a secret expedition to locate, dredge up, and sever five German telegraph cables on the floor of the North Sea to prevent the enemy from receiving news, transacting business, or spreading propaganda in America.

However, US president Woodrow Wilson believed it was important to maintain communications with Germany, in hopes of brokering a negotiated peace in Europe. The US State Department allowed the German government to send and receive messages from its embassy in Washington, DC, using America's own diplomatic telegraph service.

To communicate with the German embassy in Washington, the German foreign office first had to supply encoded messages to the American embassy in Berlin, which then sent the telegrams along via neutral Denmark and Sweden, before they finally crossed the Atlantic on an American subsea cable. The cable happened to make landfall on British soil near Land's End, where a relay station boosted the electric signal for the 3,000-mile trip across the ocean—giving British intelligence a perfect opportunity to eavesdrop on the Germans. Unbeknownst to the Germans the British had cracked their diplomatic code, thanks in part to a German cipher book captured by the Russian Navy early in the war.

On January 17, 1917, the British Admiralty's cryptography team, "Room 40," intercepted and decoded a sensational message from a member of the German Foreign Office, Arthur Zimmermann, to Count Johann von Bernstorff, the German ambassador in Washington, DC. In it, Zimmermann instructed

Bernstorff to pass a message along to Heinrich von Eckardt, the German ambassador in Mexico, offering Mexico an alliance against the United States. In return for keeping the Americans occupied while Germany finished off the Allies, Mexico would get back the lost territories of the American southwest, including Texas, New Mexico, and Arizona. If that weren't enough, the Germans also urged Mexico to enlist Japan in the proposed war against the US. The fact that the message was sent over America's own cable was the final insult.

"The thing long dreaded has come. We are virtually at war today."
—*The Los Angeles Times*

The British code-breakers at once realized the Zimmermann Telegram was a godsend. Coming on top of U-boat warfare, the German plot to embroil the US in conflict with its neighbor was sure to outrage American public opinion and finally force President Woodrow Wilson to declare war on Germany. However, before they could share the secret with the Americans, they had to conceal how they discovered it, so the Germans wouldn't figure out they'd cracked the code—and the Americans wouldn't figure out the British were eavesdropping on their diplomatic telegrams.

The head of British naval intelligence, Admiral William Hall, came up with an ingenious solution: the British would claim to have obtained a copy of the message when Bernstorff passed it along to Ambassador Eckardt in Mexico City over ordinary telegraph lines, through a British agent who bribed officials in the Mexican telegraph office (after the fact). This was the version the British showed to the Americans, who then went back over their telegraph archives and found the original copy.

The ruse worked perfectly: when Wilson released the bombshell in February 1917, it appeared the Americans were the ones who had intercepted the telegram, and the Germans ended up blaming an unknown traitor. On April 6, 1917, the US declared war on Germany—perhaps the decisive event of the war, ensuring eventual Allied victory.

61

"Uncle Sam" Artist Used Himself As the Model

Perhaps the most iconic patriotic image from America's participation in the First World War, "Uncle Sam" was James Montgomery Flagg's visualization of the American archetype for a recruiting poster—conveniently using himself as a model for the mythic character's face.

The phrase "Uncle Sam" as shorthand for the US government and America generally dates back at least to the War of 1812, and possibly earlier (the Revolutionary War song "Yankee Doodle" refers to Uncle Sam). Before the Civil War, Uncle Sam came to represent the federal government in particular and was sometimes paired with "Brother Jonathan," another figurative character representing the American people. Nineteenth-century depictions by the likes of political cartoonist Thomas Nast featured an elderly man in a patriotic suit with collar-length white hair and a goatee, but it fell to Flagg, a popular illustrator, to give Uncle Sam the instantly recognizable appearance he still bears today.

In July 1916 Flagg painted Uncle Sam for the cover of an issue of *Leslie's Weekly* using his own face as a model, with Indiana veteran Walter Botts providing the classic pose; the image appeared above a caption "What Are You Doing for Preparedness?" in reference to the national effort to prepare militarily.

The image was adapted by the US government for recruitment posters, and in 1917 and 1918, the army and other organizations printed 4 million posters featuring Uncle Sam. Uncle Sam returned to help US recruiting efforts in the Second World War, with the design of many posters essentially unchanged from two decades before. In 1944, Flagg, a fervent supporter of Franklin Delano Roosevelt, created posters showing Uncle Sam urging the president to run for his unprecedented third term.

62

The Spy Who Sort of Was Me

The name Mata Hari still conjures the female spy *par excellence*, an exotic beauty using sex to get powerful men to divulge important secrets. Except, like so much else about her, it was mostly BS.

Born Margaretha Geertruida Zelle in the Netherlands in 1876, "Margreet's" dark complexion, sometimes attributed to gypsy ancestry, gave her an exotic appearance by the standards of the day. At age eighteen she married Rudolf MacLeod, a Dutch colonial army captain stationed in the Dutch East Indies (now Indonesia), after he ran a newspaper ad seeking a European wife.

The unhappy couple had two children but MacLeod was suspicious of his beautiful young wife as well as a philanderer himself. The marriage ended in tragedy when their son died and their young daughter became gravely ill—poisoned by an aggrieved native servant, according to Margaretha, although some said their ailments were due to a sexually transmitted disease inherited from MacLeod (their daughter, Louise Jeanne MacLeod, died of congenital syphilis in 1919 at the age of twenty-one).

Margaretha Geertruida MacLeod and her volatile husband moved back to Europe but soon separated, and in 1905 she began a second career as an exotic dancer on the stages of Parisian saloons, revues, and nightclubs.

Capitalizing on her voluptuous figure and striking appearance, Margreet (as she was called) wore elaborate costumes but usually ended up nude by the end of the routines, which she claimed were based on Javanese temple dances. Recasting herself as "Mata Hari"—Malay words for the sun, literally meaning "eye of the day"—Margreet capitalized on

"Orientalism," Europe's racially tinged fascination with Asian culture, to become the first high-class, "artistic" striptease artist. In one of her most successful dances, "the veil dance," she gradually shed her clothes in front of a statue of Shiva; in another, she danced nude with a long Malay dagger.

Mata Hari's dancing caused a sensation in Parisian high society in 1905, earning her top billing at the biggest venues and launching her on a headline-making European tour (she divorced MacLeod in 1906). At the height of her popularity in the prewar years her name graced cigars and her dramatic pictures sold as popular postcards.

By 1912, however, the thirty-five-year-old dancer was already "over the hill" in the profession she had helped create, facing competition from a new generation of artistic striptease artists whom she had inspired. She made a living with some dancing, but mostly as a high-paid courtesan, sleeping with a stable of powerful men and receiving payments in return.

Caught in Germany on the outbreak of war in August 1914, Margreet relied on her relationship with a German police captain to expedite her departure, but was furious at being forced to give up all her money and belongings to leave the country. A sympathetic Dutchman bought the penniless aging star a ticket to Amsterdam, and former lovers paid the rent for a flat in The Hague.

In fall 1915 the German consul Karl Kroemer approached Mata Hari with an offer of 20,000 francs to become a German spy. According to her own account she gladly accepted the money, considering it compensation for her confiscated cash, jewelry and furs, but never intended to actually take part in espionage. However, she received a German code name, "H21," which would come back to haunt her.

In the winter of 1915–1916 Mata Hari embarked on a journey across Europe, visiting France, Spain, and Portugal in search of work, attracting the attention of both French and British intelligence officers, who sniffed around the aging performer and didn't like what they smelled. In December 1915, when her ship stopped at the British port of Folkestone, British agents interviewed her about her activities, plans, and personal life. Although they had no proof of anything amiss, Mata Hari's frank admission of a number of highly placed lovers (which at one point included the German crown prince and the Dutch prime minister) colored her as untrustworthy. The Brits had her tailed and sent a message to their French colleagues warning them to watch out for her.

Back in France she also attracted attention with a petition to visit her young lover, Captain Vladimir de Masloff, a twenty-one-year-old Russian pilot wounded on the Western Front convalescing near a sensitive military site. She appealed personally to Georges Ladoux, the head of French military intelligence, who invited her to become a spy for France (he later claimed he wanted to uncover her as an enemy spy, although he might simply have been that incompetent). Again, she eagerly accepted, lured by the promise of up to 1 million francs for good information.

In November 1916, on her first and only mission as a French operative, en route to the Netherlands Mata Hari was once again stopped at Folkestone and arrested by the British, this time in a case of mistaken identity. She asked the British to contact Ladoux to confirm that she was working for friendly French intelligence—but Ladoux disavowed Mata Hari, saying he was only trying to gather proof she was a German agent. The British prudently returned Mata Hari to Spain, where she soldiered on, seducing the German military attaché in Madrid, Major Arnold Kalle, in December 1916 in order to extract secrets in pillow talk—or so she believed. In fact, Kalle, a German intelligence officer, was probably aware of Mata Hari's current engagement by French intelligence, as well as her previous "deal" with German intelligence—which the Germans naturally considered a double cross.

Kalle apparently decided to flush out the enemy spy who'd stolen their money and double-crossed them (and perhaps rid himself of an inconvenient mistress): he sent a telegram to Berlin—using a code he most likely knew the Allies had broken—implicating Mata Hari as German spy "H21," with claims of a massive intelligence haul for Germany: "Agent H21…has arrived here. She has pretended to accept offers of service for French intelligence and to carry out trips to Belgium for the head of the service."

The frame-up worked like a charm. The intercepted German message convinced Ladoux he had been right all along, and in February 1917 the French secret service arrested Mata Hari on her return to France. The case caused a national furor when it became public knowledge, as it seemed to epitomize the French government's rampant incompetence, corruption, and stupidity. In the lurid version of events presented by prosecutors, Mata Hari used her feminine wiles to infiltrate the top echelons of France's political and military elites, stealing secrets that helped the Germans stay one step ahead at a cost of thousands of French lives.

Most of this was fantasy, but for obvious reasons none of Mata Hari's old lovers were willing to come forward to testify on her behalf. During the trial she had to admit that she accepted money from Kroemer in the Netherlands in 1915, claiming again it was restitution for her lost jewelry and furs. Despite an absence of evidence of any crime, on July 25, 1917, Mata Hari was sentenced to death. She maintained her innocence to the end. On October 15, 1917, after French president Raymond Poincaré refused a last-minute plea for clemency, she took a shot of rum, blew a kiss to someone in the crowd, and walked to face the firing squad in the moat at Vincennes. Her supposed last words: "It is unbelievable."

63

Russia's Reluctant Revolutionaries

In the years before the First World War the Russian Duma (legislative body) was dominated by liberal, pro-reform politicians who wanted more democratic representation and control of government affairs. Faced with the unbending autocracy of Nicholas II, however, nobody seems to have seriously expected things to ever change—and when a successful revolution suddenly toppled the Romanov Dynasty in March 1917, the liberal politicians were taken by surprise. The unusual result: what might be termed a reluctant revolutionary regime.

After almost three years of futile suffering and 2 million Russian dead, on March 8, 1917, tens of thousands of female workers in Petrograd went on strike to commemorate International Women's Day. The protests soon snowballed into a huge anti-war demonstration as crowds of male workers went on strike to join the women. Liberal politicians in the Duma, hoping to extract constitutional reforms, unleashed broadsides against the tsarist regime, whipping up the angry crowds up even more.

By the morning of March 9, 200,000 people were in the streets of Petrograd, and Cossack units, usually loyal to the tsar, refused to use force against them. Socialist revolutionaries distributed red banners with radical slogans and led the crowds in calls for revolution, while Tsar Nicholas II, isolated at military headquarters 500 miles away, dithered as usual. The following day the crowds grew even larger, and on March 11 the regime belatedly cracked down, with loyal troops of the Volynskii Guard Regiment opening fire on thousands of protesters in Znamenskaya Square, killing forty.

The violence only sparked fresh revolutionary fervor, fanned by Nicholas II's decision to dissolve the Duma in hopes of stifling criticism, accompanied by threats to conscript male strikers. On the evening of March 11 the mass protests morphed into a military uprising with the involvement of about half the Petrograd garrison, 160,000 strong. Imprisoning or murdering officers who refused to join them, the mutineers quickly seized control of the city amid a fair amount of bloodshed and chaos.

These were the conditions prevailing on the afternoon of March 12, when the members of the Duma's executive committee huddled with most of the rest of the Duma in a cramped antechamber of the Tauride Palace to form a new government, surrounded by an armed revolutionary crowd numbering in the tens of thousands in the streets outside. As career politicians, used to battling tsarist officialdom in speeches, not the streets, even some of the more reform-minded members were unsure whether the Duma was constitutionally allowed to deliberate if not called into session by royal decree. However, they managed to shelve these procedural concerns, thanks to a very powerful motivating factor: fear of the revolutionary mob.

As it happened the new Provisional Government, led by the idealistic but ineffectual Prince Georgy Lvov, was immediately forced to share power with the much more determined Petrograd Soviet, a mass assembly composed of deputies drawn from the ranks of socialist soldiers and workers. The Soviet's governing council consisted of the big socialist parties, including the radical Marxist Bolsheviks led by Lenin. In November 1917 the Bolsheviks, claiming to act on behalf of the Soviet, succeeded in overthrowing the weak, irrelevant Provisional Government and began remaking Russia as the Soviet Union.

64

Rising Sun in the West

After Japan declared war on Germany on August 23, 1914, Japanese naval operations extended well beyond the Pacific Ocean and Asia, as far as the Mediterranean Sea—leading to the unfamiliar sight of the Rising Sun flying over western waves.

Japanese naval cooperation with the Western Allies kicked into high gear in March 1917 with the dispatch of the Second Special Squadron, consisting of a cruiser and eight destroyers, to help the Allies with anti-submarine patrols in the Mediterranean, protecting shipping routes from the Suez Canal to Marseilles, France. Later the squadron grew to seventeen warships, including two old British destroyers manned by Japanese officers and crew.

Over the course of their deployment, the Japanese ships engaged German and Austrian U-boats on thirty-four occasions, and two of the destroyers were seriously damaged in the course of duty. One, the *Sakaki*, was torpedoed by the Austrian U-boat *U-27* with the loss of sixty-seven crewmembers, but managed to limp into port for repairs and remained in service. By the end of the war the Japanese ships had escorted 788 ships carrying over 700,000 troops through the Mediterranean.

By all accounts Japanese warships in the Mediterranean impressed—and perhaps unnerved—European observers with their high standard of training and discipline, prompting Winston Churchill to remark he "did not think that the Japanese had ever done a foolish thing." The American diplomat Kermit Roosevelt, nephew of Teddy Roosevelt, recorded his experience aboard the Japanese destroyer *Umi* as it hunted enemy submarines in the Mediterranean in 1918: "The traditional Japanese efficiency was well borne out by the speed with which our crew prepared for action. Every member was in his appointed place and the guns were stripped for action in an incredibly short time after the warning signal."

Despite the superb performance of Japanese ships, after the war the European Allies rejected Japan's request to include a statement endorsing racial equality in the Treaty of Versailles, fueling Japanese resentment of European and American arrogance (of course, the Japanese notably failed to live up to this ideal with their own Asian neighbors).

65

US Bought the Virgin Islands
to Keep U-Boats Out

One of the lesser known colonial powers, Denmark joined the European rush for sugar plantations in the Caribbean with its claim on the "Danish West Indies," later known as the Virgin Islands, in 1666. Like their colonial counterparts, Danish settlers imported African slaves to grow sugar and tobacco on the island of St. Croix, while nearby St. Thomas, with its protected harbor, made a perfect port for loading cargo (the sparsely inhabited island of St. John, with no natural source of fresh water but great scenic beauty, was a bonus).

However, the spread of sugar cultivation, falling sugar prices, and Denmark's abolition of slavery in 1803 undermined the colonial economy, and the Danish West Indies spent most of the following century in obscurity—until Germany's decision to wage U-boat warfare against Allied and neutral shipping suddenly made the tropical islands hot again.

Fearing that Germany would force its small, neutral neighbor to allow U-boats to use the Danish West Indies as a base, in October 1915 President Woodrow Wilson and Secretary of State Robert Lansing revived previous offers to buy the islands—but the Danes refused, fearing the Americans would oppress the mostly black islanders with Jim Crow–style laws. However, the Danes changed their tune after Lansing hinted they might send US troops to occupy the islands without paying; this was not an idle threat, as the Americans had recently occupied Nicaragua, Haiti, and the Dominican Republic to protect US interests (meaning business investments).

In August 1916 Lansing and the Danish ambassador, Constantin Brun, signed a treaty transferring the islands to American control for $25 million. The deal was signed by Wilson in January 1917, and the US took possession of the Danish West Indies—now renamed the Virgin Islands—on March 31, 1917, just before declaring war on Germany.

From 1917–1931 the US Navy administered the Virgin Islands as an American territory, but its inhabitants didn't enjoy legal status as US citizens until 1932, when Congress granted Virgin Islanders full citizenship (they still can't vote in presidential elections). Subsequently Laurance Rockefeller, an heir to the Standard Oil fortune, bought 5,000 acres of mostly pristine land on St. John to develop it as a resort; in 1956 he donated the land to the federal government to make a new national park.

John "Black Jack" Pershing, America's Only "General of the Armies"

Over the years America's top soldiers have held many exalted titles: George Washington was "commander in chief" of the Continental Army, a title subsequently reserved for the president of the United States. During the Civil War Ulysses S. Grant achieved the rank of "Commanding General" of the Union Army. In the modern era Dwight D. Eisenhower was appointed "Supreme Commander, Allied Expeditionary Force" in the Second World War, then later "Supreme Allied Commander" by NATO. However, in all of American history only one officer ever attained the rank of "General of the Armies."

John Joseph Pershing was a severe, disciplined career officer who received the racist epithet "Black Jack" after commanding African-American troops known as "Buffalo Soldiers" clearing Native American tribes (like many offensive nicknames, it stuck). After serving as commander of the Punitive Expedition in pursuit of the bandit leader Pancho Villa in Mexico in 1916, shortly after America's entry into the First World War, Pershing was promoted to General of the Armies, the highest possible rank that can be attained by a soldier within the US military hierarchy.

On receiving the unprecedented rank and finding himself still limited to just four stars, Pershing decided he had to distinguish himself from other four-star generals and created a new insignia with gold stars in place of the usual silver. Later, following the creation of five-star Generals of the Army during the Second World War, Pershing was informally considered a six-star general, but he passed away on July 15, 1948, age eighty-seven, before Congress could approve the new rank.

As US General of the Armies Pershing protected American sovereignty by insisting that American divisions would fight as whole units, rather than allowing them to be broken up and incorporated into the French and British armies. As the war drew to a close Pershing personally commanded the US First Army in the first phase of the victorious Meuse-Argonne Offensive from September 26 to November 11, 1918, involving 1.2 million American troops, helping break German resistance and end the war; the loss of 26,277 American lives makes it the second bloodiest battle in American history, prompting some contemporaries to criticize Pershing for incurring unnecessary casualties.

67

Half the French Army Mutinied in 1917

By the beginning of 1917, France had already suffered over a million dead plus over 2.3 million wounded, out of a prewar population of 40 million. Then in April 1917 the French launched a disastrous offensive led by General Robert Nivelle, resulting in 187,000 French casualties including another 29,000 dead, for no meaningful gains.

Now the nightmare that had haunted military leaders on both sides of the conflict finally came to pass. After almost three years of continuous bloodshed, the French Army cracked. The mutiny began on April 17, 1917, with groups of men in certain regiments refusing to go to the front lines. It soon spread to other units at the front and in reserve, ultimately affecting forty-nine divisions out of 113, or 43 percent of the French Army.

Although the spring 1917 mutinies never became a full-scale military revolt, French authorities were understandably worried: mutinying Russian soldiers had just helped overthrow the tsarist regime in March 1917, and some French mutineers were clearly inspired by the Russian Revolution.

However, most of the soldiers were simply fed up, with demands limited to fixing miserable conditions including bad food, no leave, and negligent medical services. Fortunately for the Allies, most of the mutineers were still willing to defend against German attacks—they just wouldn't make any attacks of their own.

The mutinies were so widespread there was no possibility of simply coercing soldiers back into doing their duties; the authorities had to compromise. Frantically trying to restore order before the Germans—or their own allies—found out about the breakdown in discipline, the French government fired Nivelle and elevated General Philippe Pétain, hero of the early days of Verdun, to the top spot in the French Army in May 1917.

Respected by ordinary soldiers for his care for the troops under his command, "Papa Pétain" swiftly set about listening to grievances and improving conditions; meeting with representatives from almost every unit in the French Army; and ordering more regular leave, better food, and more sympathetic medical services. But beginning in June 1917 these "carrots" were accompanied by a "stick": altogether 554 leading mutineers were sentenced to death, although the vast majority of these sentences were later commuted, with just forty-three executions carried out.

By August 1917 the mutiny was largely suppressed, but the specter of military rebellion continued to haunt both sides of the war, with good reason. In July 1917, around 9,600 Russian troops who had been sent to serve on the Western Front mutinied at La Courtine, France, but were later suppressed by Russian loyalists with heavy casualties in September. That same month British and Australian and New Zealand Army Corps (ANZAC) troops mutinied at Étaples, France, after British military police abused a soldier committing a minor infraction.

Mutinying troops played a key role in ending the war. The collapse of Germany's Hohenzollern dynasty, leading to the abdication of Kaiser Wilhelm II, began with a mutiny by German sailors in Kiel, who refused to follow their officers' suicidal orders to mount a last-minute surprise attack on the British fleet on November 3, 1918. The mutiny spread to sailors in Wilhelmshaven and was then taken up by soldiers and civilians across Germany.

68

US Trained 75,000 "Four-Minute Men"

America's entry into the First World War in April 1917 triggered a vast expansion of the US government's authority, unprecedented since the Civil War. Sweeping war measures imposed on American society over the following two years included wage and price controls; federal control of privately owned railroads, ports, and factories; and censorship of mail and news reporting.

The government wielded authority in other, less official ways, as patriotic fervor gave rise to quasi-official organizations tasked with protecting and policing the war effort. Most alarming, in 1917 Chicago advertising executive A.M. Briggs founded the American Protective League, an organization of private citizens who worked with federal, state, and local law enforcement to root out enemy spies, keep tabs on anti-war dissent, and maintain morals by closing down bars and brothels and chasing prostitutes away from towns near training camps.

Members of the APL and loosely affiliated American nativist organizations often went quite a bit further, busting up pacifist meetings, attacking striking workers, and generally behaving like thugs. Remarkably, Briggs received official authorization for the APL from US Attorney General Thomas Gregory, who boasted: "I have today several hundred thousand private citizens...assisting the heavily overworked Federal authorities in keeping an eye on disloyal individuals and making reports of disloyal utterances." At its height the APL counted over 250,000 members in 600 cities across the US, although their degree of active involvement varied.

However, America's leaders understood it wasn't simply a matter of suppressing dissent: they also needed to take positive steps to mold public opinion in support of the government's war effort and aims. Toward that end, on April 14, 1917—just over a week into the war—President Wilson authorized the creation of the Committee on Public Information, a propaganda machine under the control of George Creel, a well-known investigative journalist turned politician, who headed up the effort to convince Americans that the war was just and the US government's war effort a glowing success.

Creel created a structure of thirty-seven divisions, each focused on a major medium or key topic, including a news PR machine; a department for "pictorial publicity," which churned out recruitment posters, buttons, cartoons, and billboards; and a film division, riding the wave of popular cinema.

At the Movies

In an era before TV or radio, going to movies was a regular habit for many Americans. In 1914 around 7 million Americans went to the movies every day, increasing to 10 million by 1917 and 12.5 million by 1920.

But delivering propaganda via the spoken word was more difficult in an age before widespread adoption of radio (America's first commercial broadcast didn't debut until November 1920). The CPI distributed phonograph records of Wilson's speeches and other pro-war content, but it still needed to reach large numbers of people, impromptu, in public situations with short, timely messages—so it created a sort of human public address system, the "Four-Minute Men."

The Four-Minute Men consisted of around 75,000 volunteers—mostly men, but with a good number of female speakers—who were trained to give quick, self-contained speeches voicing support for the war effort, up to four minutes long. Whenever possible the speakers were recruited from among a community's notable figures, including respected businessmen, fire and law enforcement, teachers, and clergy of all religions, whose local knowledge allowed them to tailor speeches for specific audiences.

From 1917 to 1918, the Four-Minute Men delivered a total of 7,555,910 speeches on a variety of subjects to audiences in venues such as town hall meetings, theater performances, sports matches, galas, and exhibitions. The speakers were often rotated on local and regional circuits to keep audiences engaged with fresh messages. The ranks of the Four-Minute Men (and women) included legendary comedian Charlie Chaplin, silent film heartthrob and action star Douglas Fairbanks, and Hollywood beauty Mary Pickford, who married Fairbanks in 1920.

"The Loudest Sound in History"

One of the largest manmade non-nuclear explosions in human history occurred in the early morning of June 7, 1917, during the opening of the Battle of Messines in Belgium, when British attackers detonated a series of huge mines under the German trenches, producing a blast audible in neighboring countries. In fact, the British Prime Minister, David Lloyd George, supposedly heard the blast 140 miles away, across the English Channel.

The British offensive at Messines aimed to capture strategic high ground southeast of Ypres, giving them artillery positions for an even bigger attack to follow later that summer at the Third Battle of Ypres, also known as Passchendaele. The plan of attack included the construction of twenty-two mines under the German lines, some requiring tunnels hundreds of meters long, excavated over many months by engineers working from concealed positions. The mines were packed with a total of 454 tons (almost a million pounds) of ammonal high explosive and gun cotton, including three mines containing over 90,000 pounds of explosive each.

"Gentlemen, we may not make history tomorrow, but we shall certainly change the geography."
—*Charles Harington, chief of staff, British Second Army*

At 3:10 a.m. on the morning of June 7, 1917, British sappers detonated the explosives by electric signals, sending up nineteen mines (three failed due to technical problems). In a few moments the massive combined explosion killed around 10,000 German soldiers, and together with a punishing artillery bombardment set the stage for a successful British advance over the following days.

Ammonal is about half the strength of TNT, so the mines detonated at Messines would have been equal to around a quarter of a kiloton in the metric used for nuclear weapons (by comparison the Little Boy device dropped on Hiroshima was equivalent to 16 kilotons of TNT). In the city of Lille, located 12 miles away, the rocking earth triggered fears of an earthquake, and the next day *The Times* of London reported that Lloyd George said he heard the explosions at his home in Surrey.

Some skeptics argue that Lloyd George did indeed hear massive explosions from the beginning of the Battle of Messines—but that the "boom" was actually the British artillery barrage, timed to coincide with the mine explosion.

70

Russia's All-Women "Battalion of Death"

By general agreement in early twentieth-century Europe, war was strictly a man's domain, with women's roles limited to nursing wounded men, gathering donations, and other functions behind the front. However, there were exceptions, most notably in Russia, where the Provisional Government agreed to create an all-female "Battalion of Death."

The Battalion of Death was founded and led by Maria Leontievna Bochkareva, a Siberian peasant woman who fought under the nom de guerre "Yashka." After war broke out in 1914, Bochkareva left her abusive husband and asked to join the 25th Tomsk Reserve Battalion, a Siberian unit, but the male officers laughed off the suggestion. She then petitioned Tsar Nicholas II, who granted her request.

Unsurprisingly male soldiers often greeted the sight of a female soldier with surprise and scorn, but most skeptics were won over by Yashka's remarkable personal bravery, physical endurance, attention to the wounded, and consideration for the men under her command. After rescuing fifty men, Yashka was promoted to corporal, in charge of eleven men in the frontline trenches, and participated in major battles, including an ill-fated Russian offensive in what is now Lithuania in March 1916:

The signal to advance was given, and we started, knee-deep in mud, for the enemy. In places the pools reached above our waists. Shells and bullets played havoc among us. Of those who fell wounded, many sank in the mud and were drowned. The German fire was devastating. Our lines grew thinner and thinner, and progress became so slow that our doom was certain…

Nor was she entirely alone, as Russia had a long if mostly unacknowledged tradition of female fighters. A number of women appear to have succeeded in joining by disguising themselves as men, at least in the early days of the war. John Morse, an Englishman serving with the Russian Army, noted in 1915:

There are peculiarities in all peoples: and one of those of the Russians is the number of females serving in their ranks, many of them as officers. Indeed, I heard that one lady commanded a regiment of Cossacks!... I saw some of these female soldiers—quite a score in all. There was nothing particularly romantic in the appearance of any of them... One girl, said to be only eighteen years old, was quite six feet high, with limbs that would fit a grenadier.

Even more women fought for the Russian Army after the March 1917 revolution, when War Minister Alexander Kerensky agreed to Yashka's proposal to form an all-women's unit to combat demoralization in the ranks—in part by shaming male soldiers to fight. In June 1917 Bochkareva formed the 1st Russian Women's Battalion of Death, having whittled around 2,000 applicants down to 300 committed female warriors. The battalion was consecrated in Petrograd's St. Isaac's Cathedral in a public ceremony where Yashka was presented with a banner from Kerensky, then carried by cheering soldiers and sailors on their shoulders.

Bochkareva's "Battalion of Death" and another battalion from Perm both took part in combat at the front, including a successful temporary advance during the doomed Kerensky Offensive of July 1917. They also played a key role in the unsuccessful defense of the Provisional Government against the Bolshevik coup in November 1917: the 2nd Moscow Women's Battalion of Death was the last army unit guarding the Winter

Palace, the seat of the Provisional Government. Overall 5,000 women volunteered to fight in the various all-female units under the Provisional Government.

While they rendered honorable service, the women's battalions seemed to have had little of their intended effect on men's morale: after three long years of indescribable misery, exhausted Russian soldiers were no longer susceptible to shame. Shortly after taking power Lenin's Bolsheviks dissolved the women's battalions, suspicious of any rival armed organization. However, female soldiers later fought on both the "Red" and "White" sides of the Russian Civil War.

Yashka herself was no friend to the Bolsheviks. In 1918 they accused her of conspiring with White General Lavr Kornilov, but she managed to escape Russia via Vladivostok to the United States. She was granted a personal meeting with Woodrow Wilson in July 1918, begging him to intervene in Russia on humanitarian grounds (US troops eventually occupied the Russian ports of Vladivostok and Archangel). After dictating her memoirs in New York City, she traveled to Britain to meet with King George V.

In April 1919 Yashka returned to Tomsk, Siberia, to serve in a medical unit under White General Alexander Kolchak. She was caught and executed by the *Cheka,* the Bolshevik secret police, on May 16, 1920.

71

British Royal Family Changed Its Name to "Windsor"

During the First World War Britain was seized by an anti-German fever, and restaurants, stores, and other businesses with "German" names were forced to adopt new "English" ones or succumb to boycotts, even if the owners were British-born. It wasn't just symbolic changes: in October 1914 the navy's First Sea Lord, Prince Louis of Battenberg, was forced to resign his post because of his German and Austrian background, made obvious by his name.

Most awkward of all, however, was the fact that the British royal family themselves were largely of German descent. Britain had first imported German royalty with the ascent of George Louis, elector of Hanover, to the throne as King George I in 1715 after the death of his second cousin Queen Anne, initiating the Hanoverian line of British kings. The royal family got another infusion of German blood in 1840, when the young Queen Victoria married Prince Albert, son of the Duke of Saxe-Coburg and Gotha. Although Queen Victoria kept her family name as a member of the House of Hanover, her successors Edward VII and George V took the name of their father's noble house.

While their loyalty was not in question, the fact that the British royal family bore the German name Saxe-Coburg and Gotha was not exactly ideal, especially after German Gotha heavy bombers began raiding Britain in early 1917. Thus on July 17, 1917, King George V issued a decree changing the British royal family's name from Saxe-Coburg and Gotha to Windsor, after the town that is the seat of the royal family's main residence at Windsor Castle. In addition, the royals gave up all their German titles and positions—Prince Battenberg became Lord Mountbatten—and the king stripped his German relations of their British titles.

Not everyone was impressed by the nominal change. Thomas Hope Floyd, a British officer, wrote in a letter home:

I am rather amused at the change in the Royal Name: our Royal Family is now to be known as the Royal House of Windsor! It does strike me as pandering somewhat to popular prejudice. That King George should change his name to Windsor cannot change the fact of his ancestry; he is still a member of the Royal House of Coburg...no legal document can alter the facts of heredity!

72

The Flight of the L-59

From 1914–1918 German East Africa (today Tanzania) was the scene of one of the most successful guerrilla warfare campaigns in military history, as a tiny force of European and native soldiers led by German commander Paul Emil von Lettow-Vorbeck eluded and defeated larger Allied armies time and again.

Although the final outcome was never in doubt, the guerrilla campaign counted as a victory simply by preventing huge numbers of Allied troops from serving elsewhere. Over the course of the war a total of 34,000 German regular and irregular troops, typically organized in armies of just a few thousand each, managed to tie up Allied forces numbering 250,000 soldiers (along with 600,000 porters).

On November 21, 1917, the specially modified Imperial German Navy zeppelin L-59 embarked on the longest airship journey of the war in a bold attempt to resupply Lettow-Vorbeck. With an extra-large 743-foot-long hydrogen gasbag, a cargo capacity of 14 tons, and a top speed of 64 miles per hour, the "Africa Ship" was packed with critical necessities including thirty machine guns, ammunition, replacement parts, food, and medical supplies as well as a medical team. It carried 22 tons of fuel, only enough to make a one-way trip, so on reaching Africa the crew of twenty-two would join Lettow-Vorbeck's troops, and the zeppelin itself would be broken up and its components repurposed as a radio station, tents, boots, and uniforms, among other necessities.

Flying from an airbase at Yamboli, Bulgaria, under captain Ludwig Bockholt, the L-59 headed south across the Mediterranean Sea and north Africa in taxing conditions for the crew, who suffered extreme cold, dizziness, and oxygen deprivation. Each of the zeppelin's five engines was rested for maintenance for two out of every ten hours in rotation, with five dedicated mechanics always in attendance. Over Africa the airship became unstable when the tropical sun heated the gasbags at high altitudes, and encountered extreme turbulence from thermals at lower altitudes, almost crashing; the crew also complained of being blinded by the reflection of the sun on the Sahara Desert.

Despite losing one engine to mechanical trouble the zeppelin continued its voyage, making it as far as British Sudan before receiving a faint radio signal from Germany with an order to abort the mission: it turned out that Lettow-Vorbeck's dwindling forces had been pushed out of the plains where the L-59 was supposed to land, into mountainous terrain where tethering the buoyant airship would be all but impossible. Although his crew begged him to continue, Bockholt obeyed orders and flew back to Bulgaria, dumping most of the cargo to maintain lift. The flight of the L-59 had lasted four days and covered a total distance of 4,200 miles. The zeppelin was later destroyed while on patrol duty over the Mediterranean on April 7, 1918.

Meanwhile Lettow-Vorbeck abandoned East Africa and invaded Portuguese Mozambique, where he found plentiful supplies to support his continued guerrilla campaign for the rest of the war. He finally surrendered, undefeated, on November 25, 1918.

73

The World Gets Jazz, Really Gets It, Man

"Not many weeks ago I had my first experience of a Jazz band, while taking afternoon-tea in a well-known West End tea-room," music critic Francesco Berger wrote in 1919, continuing:

> It was one of the strongest and strangest experiences I have undergone in an extended life, during which I have listened to much that was good, more that was bad, and to most that was indifferent. It produced an impression that was not quite pleasant, but not entirely unpleasant, a sort of comical mixture of both... Pleasurable though staggering, making it difficult to recover one's breath, defying analysis, repellent at the outset, but magnetically fascinating.

The early history of African-American jazz music is rife with legend and anecdote, but hard facts are considerably fewer. In the early twentieth century the American popular music scene was firmly in the grips of ragtime mania, with white audiences clamoring for the syncopated or "ragged" musical style originating in the black communities of river towns of the upper South and Midwest, popularized by musicians including Scott Joplin and "Jelly Roll" Morton. By 1915, however, the African-American musical scene was already moving to a compelling new sound. At some point in the decade before the war African-American and Creole musicians in New Orleans, Chicago, and elsewhere began experimenting with a wildly improvisational musical style marrying polyrhythmic tempos with rollicking piano and exuberant brass horns. Like most new forms of music, jazz most likely had multiple origins, including Creole musical styles of the Caribbean; some historians speculate African-American musicians were influenced by exposure to Afro-Cuban music during the Spanish-American War.

Whatever its exact musical roots, jazz was a world-shaking phenomenon. Like the blues and ragtime before it, the new sound first spread through the black communities of the Midwestern river valleys, before being brought to the rest of the country by African Americans leaving the Jim Crow South in search of industrial work in the North during the First World War.

Jazz bands first appeared in the clubs of Chicago's South Side by 1915, and in October 1916 *Variety* magazine made its first mention of "Jass bands." White musicians were quick to pick up the new style: in 1917 the Original Dixieland Jazz Band, an all-white outfit that was arguably none of those things, recorded the first jazz record and took New York City by storm with their hit "Livery Stable Blues."

As more black and white musicians jumped on the bandwagon, the irresistible new sound followed American soldiers across the Atlantic to France and Britain. In fact, some pioneering jazz bands were already touring Europe. In 1917 the French poet Jean Cocteau marveled after seeing a jazz performance featuring an array of percussion instruments: "To the right of the little group dressed in black, there was a barman of noises under a gilt pergola laden with bells, rods, boards, and motorcycle horns. From them, he made cocktails adding from time to time a dash of cymbals, rising, swaying and smiling beatifically."

The experience of performing in Europe was eye opening for young musicians used to overt, institutionally entrenched racism in America. One musician, Louis Mitchell, wrote home breathlessly from Britain in August 1918, "this is the finest Country in the world and if you once get over here you will never want to go back to N.Y. again. I intend to stay here for the rest of my life, as you can go where you want too [sic] and have the time of your life…"

Jazz got an even bigger boost in Europe when several segregated African-American units created military bands with talented musicians who performed jazz hits, along with other types of popular music, for military and civilian audiences. One such band, formed by the 15th New York Infantry, and led by the appropriately named James Reese Europe, counted forty-four members and provided entertainment for off-duty troops as well as serving as America's musical emissary in Europe. Sergeant Noble Sissle recalled one performance:

> Then it seemed the whole audience began to sway: dignified French officers began to pat their feet in time with the American general, who temporarily lost his style and grace… At the signal, in the perfect unison, the whole [trombone] section threw their slides to the extremity and jerked them back with an ear-splitting crack…and the audience could not stand the strain any longer: the "Jazz germ" hit them…

William Russel, an American soldier in the air force supply service, wrote home about another performance by an American revue on January 25, 1918: "They had an American Jazz band, which is the hit of the show. The French people simply go wild over it."

In 1920 the alternative record label OKeh recorded the first record by an African-American performer, Mamie Smith, and by 1925 "race records" by black performers were selling up to 6 million records a year. Not everyone was enamored of the new sound, however, and the views of many white Americans and Europeans were inevitably colored by racist attitudes.

Beginning in the 1920s the Nazis condemned jazz as "degenerate" music associated with inferior races, and in the 1930s targeted "swing" music popular among some youth subcultures. Nevertheless the 1920s was undoubtedly the age of jazz music, and its popularity only grew in decades to come with the spread of "swing" jazz and numerous other genres.

74

Horrible Accidents Killed Thousands of People

In addition to all the deliberate bloodshed during the First World War, thousands of people were killed by accidents, the inevitable result of inherently unsafe conditions at the front, with the movement of large numbers of men and high explosives in close proximity, as well as lax industrial and civil safety standards at home.

Fort Douaumont. After falling to the Germans without a fight in the opening days of the attack on Verdun in February 1916, Fort Douaumont became the nerve center of the German Army's logistics and communications behind the front. Thousands of men heading to the front or into reserves passed through Fort Douaumont, along with a prodigious amount of high explosives and ammunition. From February to July 1916, forty-three German divisions, or about a third of the German Army, fought at Verdun, most of them passing through the fort. On May 8, 1916, disaster struck when a cooking fire came in contact with spilled flamethrower fluid, eventually causing three huge explosions that rocked the fort, which, however, remained standing. Accidents with friendly fire added to the disaster, which left 679 German soldiers dead. Remarkably the Germans managed to conceal the magnitude of the accident from the French.

Tavannes Tunnel. Coincidentally the French suffered an almost parallel disaster at Verdun. Less than five kilometers east of Verdun, the French Army had converted a large disused 1,000-meter rail tunnel near Fort Tavannes into a supply depot, rest area, and hospital. According to one account, the disaster on September 4, 1916, occurred when an ammunition supply mule came too close to a cooking fire, igniting rocket flares in its side bags.

This caused the agitated animal to run down the tunnel, where it ignited messy tins of gasoline, which in turn ignited ammunition. Whatever the cause, the explosion, fire, and smoke killed over 500 French troops in just a few minutes. This time the Germans were left clueless.

Halifax. On December 6, 1917, the *Imo*, a Norwegian ship chartered to carry relief supplies to Belgium, accidentally collided with the *Mont-Blanc*, a French ship carrying around 3,000 tons of volatile high explosives. A fire sparked by spilled benzol on the *Mont-Blanc* quickly grew out of control, and around twenty minutes after the collision the ship's cargo exploded with a force equivalent to 2.9 kilotons of TNT. The massive blast wave, traveling at over 1,000 meters a second, completely destroyed 1,600 houses and damaged 12,000 more, and also triggered a 35-foot-tall tidal wave in Halifax Harbor, inundating the city's Richmond district and wiping out a local First Nations community. In ten seconds the explosion and tidal wave killed over 2,000 people and injured 9,000 more.

Salonika. In fall 1915 the French and British occupied the port city of Salonika in northern Greece in a vain attempt to send reinforcements to Serbia, facing invasion from three sides. Although they failed in this mission, the Allies continued to occupy northern Greece, where they faced Central Powers on the "Macedonian" front until the end of the war. Cramming hundreds of thousands of soldiers and refugees into an ancient, neglected city of 150,000 people was not exactly safe. At around 3:00 p.m. on August 18, 1917, a refugee family's cooking fire got out control and ignited a pile of straw. The conflagration spread quickly thanks to a strong, steady wind, and over the course of thirty-two hours around half the city burned to the ground, destroying 9,500 homes over an area of around one square kilometer and leaving 70,000 homeless. The disaster was compounded by the fact that Salonika had no formal fire brigade, while the Allies had taken control of the city's water supply for their own needs.

Industrial Accidents. On both sides of the conflict, accidental explosions in munitions factories and other industrial accidents killed thousands of people over the course of the war. In Britain alone 600 workers and nearby residents perished in accidents in war industries, including 109 boys and men killed by an explosion in Faversham, Kent, on April 2, 1916; 45 women and girls killed in Leeds on December 5, 1916; 73 killed at Silvertown in East London on January 19, 1917; 43 killed when a TNT plant blew up at Ashton-under-Lyne, near Manchester, on June 13, 1917; and 134 killed in Chilwell, Nottingham, on July 1, 1918. On May 22, 1915, the worst rail accident in British history occurred at Quintinshill, near the huge new Gretna Green arms factory in Dumfriesshire, Scotland, killing over 200 people.

PART 6

1918: The Bitter End

UNLIKE THE SECOND World War, which mostly saw slow but steady progress by the Allies from 1942 onwards, the First World War was a nail biter right up to the end. As 1918 began it was by no means clear that the Allies were going to win the war: Europe's fate hinged on the outcome of the mighty German spring offensive, intended to break the Allies on the Western Front before American troops could start arriving in large numbers.

Erich Ludendorff, Germany's top strategist, identified the weak point in the Allied line with his usual precision. On March 21, 1918, the German Second, Seventeenth, and Eighteenth Armies pounded the British Third and Fifth Armies with unprecedented firepower, and by March 28 the British Fifth Army was all but destroyed—the most serious British defeat of the war. But French reinforcements helped hold the German offensive to the south, while the British Third Army regrouped. By early April the first German offensive had failed.

Four more offensives would follow, gradually diminishing in power, as Ludendorff sought desperately to achieve a decisive breakthrough by the summer, when American troops started to arrive in Europe in huge numbers. From 329,000 in March 1918 the total number of US troops jumped to 1.2 million by July 1918, the date of Ludendorff's last offensive, and 2 million by October.

American manpower turned the tables decisively in favor of the Allies, and by August 1918 German armies were in retreat along the Western Front, as the new Allied supreme commander, Marshal Ferdinand Foch, unleashed the "Hundred Days Offensive." On September 30, 1918, Bulgaria begged for peace, while Damascus fell to Arab and British forces on October 1. On the Italian front, Allied forces prepared to stage a final successful offensive at Vittorio Veneto, triggering the collapse of the Austro-Hungarian Army and with it Austria-Hungary itself.

With defeat looming, on October 4, 1918, the new German chancellor, Max von Baden, sent a telegraph to US president Woodrow Wilson requesting peace negotiations. Over the next month the American president issued a number of demands, including the immediate evacuation of all occupied territory and the creation of a democratic government in Germany. On October 28 German sailors in Kiel mutinied, triggering the German Revolution, followed by the abdication of Kaiser Wilhelm II and the creation of a new government dominated by socialists (which the military cleverly made take the blame for the unfair Treaty of Versailles).

On the "eleventh hour of the eleventh day of the eleventh month" (November 11) the armistice went into effect on the Western Front, and the guns went silent across Europe.

75

The "Paris Gun" and America's Plans for a Supergun

After forcing Russia to make peace at Brest-Litovsk, in spring 1918 Germany transferred over a million troops from the Eastern Front for a final series of attempts to defeat the Allies on the Western Front before American reinforcements began to arrive. The five spring offensives ultimately failed to break through the Allied lines, but they did bring German troops close enough to the French capital to deploy seven "superguns" that could drop shells on targets over 75 miles away.

The biggest artillery piece of the war in terms of barrel length (not to be confused with Krupp's 420-millimeter "Big Bertha" howitzer, the biggest by caliber) the Paris Guns were repurposed naval pieces that required eighty sailors of the Imperial German Navy to assemble and operate. Over 111 feet long, each gun weighed 256 tons and was transported in pieces by rail for assembly on a fixed circular mounting with a concrete foundation. With a crane-like support structure, it was capable of firing a 211-millimeter (later 238-millimeter) shell weighing 234 pounds up to 81 miles, reaching a maximum altitude of 26.3 miles, well into the stratosphere. The shell took just over three minutes to travel to its target.

Of course, "targets" were highly imprecise, given the distance involved, which made aerial reconnaissance for artillery spotting difficult. The guns could hit Paris from their first emplacements at the forest of Coucy, but the Germans were largely unable to target specific neighborhoods or districts. Additionally, the thick steel shells, heavily reinforced to survive reentry, could only carry a small 15-pound high-explosive charge, making them less destructive than regular shells of comparable size. The high muzzle velocity also wore down the interior of the barrel quickly, requiring precise measurements and adjustments lasting over an hour before it could be fired again.

Despite these limitations the gun caused understandable confusion and fear when it began shelling Paris on the morning of March 21, 1918. The shells continued to arrive at a rate of up to 20 per day, with a total of at least 320 fired by August 1918, when the Allied counterattack forced the Germans back. The long-distance shelling killed a total of 250 people and wounded 620 more, in addition to destroying or damaging a large amount of property. In the deadliest incident, on March 29, 1918, Good Friday, a shell caused a church roof to collapse on the congregation during services, killing ninety-one.

The Paris Guns accomplished nothing of military value and failed to trigger panic among civilians in Paris, while provoking yet more criticism of the German military on moral and humanitarian grounds.

"If only we could accompany a shell on its course, we should find a strange condition of affairs. The higher we rose, the darker would the heavens become, until the sun would shine like a fiery ball in a black sky. All around, the stars would twinkle, and below would be the glare of light reflected from the earth's surface and its atmosphere, while the cold would be far more intense than anything suffered on earth. Up at that height, there would be nothing to indicate that the shell was moving—no rush of air against the ears. We should seem detached from earth and out in the endless reaches of space."

—*Alexander Russell Bond, managing editor,* Scientific American

Meanwhile in 1918 the US Army Ordnance Office also toyed around with the idea of an even bigger supergun (happily never built). The American super-long-range artillery piece would have had a barrel 225 feet long, assembled from four sections and supported by a long steel truss, weighing a total of 325 tons. With an explosive firing charge weighing 1,440 pounds, it could have fired a 10-inch, 400-pound shell to a range of up to 121.3 miles, or about the distance from New York City to Wilmington, Delaware. The shell would have had a flight time of four minutes and nine seconds, reaching a maximum altitude of 46 miles—the edge of space.

US Built the First Pilotless Drone

Nowadays even amateur enthusiasts have access to remote-controlled drones, but a century ago they were the stuff of science fiction. While it wasn't much use during the war—or afterward—America still gets credit for developing the world's first pilotless drone.

The government-funded project for the US Army aircraft board brought together legendary aviation pioneer Orville Wright and Charles Kettering, founder of Dayton Engineer Laboratories Company, or Delco, an electrical engineering firm bought by General Motors. In 1918 Wright served as an aeronautical consultant on Kettering's design for a "self-flying aerial torpedo," built by the Dayton-Wright Airplane Company, which the army hoped would enable long-range attacks on enemy fortifications, facilities, or ships.

A biplane built of laminate wood, papier-mâché, and cardboard, measuring 12 feet long with a 15-foot wingspan, the "Kettering Bug" weighed in at a trim 530 pounds and was powered by one 40-horsepower Ford motor (for comparison, the Liberty engine mass-produced by American manufacturers for piloted planes during the war produced 449 horsepower). Obviously, this meant the Bug was rather slow, with a top speed of 50 miles per hour, but speed was less important when no lives were at risk, and the aircraft itself was fairly cheap to build at $400.

The Bug could carry a bomb weighing up to 180 pounds and had a maximum range of 75 miles, further than most artillery of the day. The main obstacle was steering and targeting: while the First World War saw the first use of wireless radio to communicate with pilots, the technology was nowhere near sophisticated enough to enable remote control.

Kettering came up with a straightforward solution: the Bug would fly in a certain direction to a preset distance as measured by the number of propeller revolutions, then automatically drop its wings and payload.

The first test flight on October 2, 1918, failed when the prototype Bug climbed too steeply and stalled, but it later flew successfully on seven out of twenty-four attempts. The army worried the Bug might accidentally drop its bomb on Allied troops, but there was more interest in its potential for targeting ships over open water. A total of forty-five Bugs were built, but with the war over, funding was terminated in March 1920.

While often described as a drone, some skeptics argue the Bug is better classified as an early cruise missile. Indeed, it foreshadowed the V-1 flying bomb developed by Nazi Germany in 1939, which rained terror on England and Belgium during the Second World War; like the Bug, the V-1 was simply designed to fly a certain distance and then drop (when it ran out of fuel) making it highly imprecise.

Fighting Across Siberia:
The Czech Legion's Amazing Escape

The incredible story of 40,000 former Czech and Slovak prisoners of war who fought their way across Siberia during the Russian Civil War has few parallels in history. The Czech Legion was living proof of the dissolution of the Austro-Hungarian Empire. Most of its fighters were Czech and Slovakian peasants drafted into the Habsburg Army and sent unwillingly to fight their fellow Slavs, the Russians, on the Eastern Front. After deserting or being captured, disaffected Czech and Slovak soldiers were recruited from the POW camps by Russian intelligence to form a nationalist Czech Legion, in return for an Allied promise to support Czech independence from Austria.

> "We, the Czechoslovak soldiers of the first revolutionary army beyond our nation's borders, hereby break our contractual ties with the Habsburgs and the Austro-Hungarian monarchy, remembering those great and thus far not vindicated wrongs, which they perpetrated for entire centuries on our dear Czechoslovak nation..."
> —*Czech Legion oath*

As traitors to the Habsburg crown, members of the Czech Legion believed they would be severely punished if captured by loyalists and fought bravely against their former compatriots in the Kerensky Offensive in July 1917. However, their situation became more complicated when Lenin's Bolsheviks overthrew the Provisional Government in November 1917. As Russia descended into the chaos of civil war the Czech Legion, still loyal to the Allies, suddenly found themselves isolated in a huge, unfriendly country. The Allies hoped to deploy the Legion to counter Germany's final spring offensives on the Western Front, but the Central Powers blocked the short route across Europe—so they would have to go the long way round.

The very long way around: the Allied plan called for the Czech Legion, retreating before the advancing Germans in Ukraine in February 1918, to leave Russia by traveling 6,000 miles east on the Trans-Siberian Railroad to Russia's Pacific port of Vladivostok, then back to Europe through the Indian Ocean and Mediterranean.

In May 1918 the Czechs, heading east, encountered Austrian and Hungarian POWs heading west to be repatriated to Austria-Hungary following the Treaty of Brest-Litovsk, leading to violent clashes between the rival groups. Local Bolshevik officials tried to crack down on the Czech Legion following these incidents, but heavy-handed tactics sparked a revolt among the Czechs, who seized control of the city of Chelyabinsk, a large Siberian city located about 1,000 miles east of Moscow, and an important stop on the strategic Trans-Siberian Railroad.

Taking over hundreds of trains, the Czech Legion fanned out along the railroad, sending train-based battalions to storm rail stations and toss the Bolsheviks out of other key cities including Tomsk, Samara, and Vladivostok by the end of June 1918. In keeping with this new style of warfare, they turned their fleets of trains into self-contained traveling bases, complete with barracks, canteens, bakeries, hospitals, and repair shops. The Legion's passenger and supply trains were protected by formidable armored trains, which also led the advance into enemy territory.

In the vast, sparsely populated wilderness of Siberia, only partially occupied by small forces focused on scattered cities, the 30,000 troops of the Czech Legion were a formidable foe, and they cannily exploited their control of communications, including all-important telephone and tele-graph lines, to surprise and outwit their enemies. Remarkably, the Czech Legion published their own newspaper and operated their own postal system in the cities along the Trans-Siberian Railroad.

The Czech Legion continued controlling portions of the Trans-Siberian Railroad until April 1920, when amid the collapse of White Russian forces they were finally evacuated by the British, Japanese, and Americans from Russia's Pacific port of Vladivostok. On returning home the Czech Legion's veterans were hailed as heroes whose sacrifices helped earn Allied support for Czechoslovakian independence. They established their own bank and played an important role in the new nation's civic institutions in the interwar years.

US Troops Occupied Large Parts of Russia

After the Russian Civil War broke out in late 1917, the Allies intervened in an attempt to help the anti-Bolshevik "White armies" fight "the Reds," occupying Russian territory to secure ports and railroads and protect weapons and other supplies from falling into the hands of Leon Trotsky's Red Army.

Initially reluctant to involve American troops in a new conflict, in July 1918 President Woodrow Wilson finally relented, persuaded by the need to help the stranded Czech Legion (and keep an eye on Japan's occupation of Russia's Far East with 70,000 troops). Two months later two American forces landed at opposite ends of the vast Russian landmass, one occupying Archangel, a key northern port on the White Sea, the other landing in Vladivostok, Russia's main Pacific port.

On September 4, 1918, 5,000 soldiers in the American North Russian Expeditionary Force (most of the troops, nicknamed "Polar Bears," were enlistees from Michigan) landed in Archangel, where their main mission was guarding war supplies. But the Bolsheviks beat them to the punch, removing most of the munitions before the Allies landed. In a classic case of "mission creep" the American troops, now under British command, ended up fighting Red Army forces alongside British troops, in one case pushing the Bolsheviks back hundreds of miles along the north Russian Vologda railroad.

These offensives soon petered out due to Russia's sheer size, which had defeated so many previous invaders, and by October 1918 the Anglo-American force withdrew to more easily defended positions guarding the approach to Archangel. After almost a year in Russia's far north, in June 1919 the Polar Bears were finally withdrawn and sent home to America. They were replaced by 8,000 British troops, who continued occupying Archangel until the end of the Allied north Russia intervention in March 1920. Two hundred twenty-six Americans died of various causes during the Polar Bear Expedition, around half of whom were buried in Russia; most of these bodies were later repatriated, with many buried around a monument to the Polar Bears in Troy, Michigan. Around thirty US servicemen remain buried in Russia.

Meanwhile the 7,950 men of the American Expeditionary Force Siberia, nicknamed the "Wolfhounds," began arriving in Vladivostok on August 15, 1918, with the mission of guarding the strategic Trans-Siberian Railroad north of the city; this also meant operating the railroad, for which a special military bureau was formed, the US Army's Russian Railway Service Corps.

Unlike the Polar Bears in Archangel, the Wolfhounds remained under American command and therefore avoided major combat with the Red Army or other civil war factions. However, the Russian Far East was primitive and isolated, and American soldiers suffered acutely from cold, shortage of food and fuel, and disease. By the time they were finally withdrawn from Siberia on April 1, 1920, the Wolfhounds had suffered 189 deaths. Most of their remains were transported back to the US via San Francisco in 1920.

79

Gandhi Supported the British War Effort

The pacifist who led the struggle for Indian independence from the British Empire started out in a very different place: in fact Mohandas Gandhi supported the British war effort during the First World War, reasoning that the British would repay India's help with autonomy afterward.

Gandhi first became politically active in South Africa, where he worked as a civil rights lawyer representing the local Indian community, most descendants of manual laborers brought over by the British in the nineteenth century. Educated at a British law school, during this period Gandhi wore Western suits and espoused the virtues of British justice—even though it was clearly lacking in South Africa, where Indians were treated as second-class citizens.

Concluding it was just a problem of applying British law to the rest of the empire, Gandhi filed lawsuits, organized boycotts and protests, and called on support from Hindu and Muslim community leaders to force South Africa's government to live up to British ideals—getting arrested countless times along the way. But at this stage his idealism applied only to Indians, with no mention of civil rights for black South Africans.

Two days after the assassination of Archduke Franz Ferdinand in Sarajevo, Gandhi's hard work finally paid off: on June 30, 1914, the governor of South Africa, Jan Smuts, signed an agreement guaranteeing the legal rights of Indians living in South Africa. His work in South Africa done, on July 18 he boarded a steamship for Britain—only to find the world teetering on the brink of war when he arrived.

"India would be nowhere without Englishmen. If the British do not win, to whom shall we go claiming equal partnership? Shall we go to the victorious German or Turk or Afghan for it? The liberty-loving English will surely yield after seeing that we have laid down our lives for them."
—*Gandhi, July 1918*

Gandhi initially hoped to achieve reforms and win concessions that would give India equality within the British Empire—which meant supporting the British war effort. After returning to India, he started organizing civil rights campaigns that landed him in jail (again) and founded an *ashram*, or commune, including members of India's "untouchable" underclass. But in 1918 he also agreed to help the colonial regime recruit Indian soldiers to serve in Europe and the Middle East.

Gandhi believed that by creating a large native military force, India would gain leverage to demand home rule after the war, and he pointed out that Indian troops "trained for fighting will be able to wrest freedom in a moment," and "even fight the Empire, should it play foul with us." But he still favored home rule within the British Empire over full independence.

His attitude only started to change in April 1919 following the Amritsar Massacre, when British troops killed at least 379 unarmed protesters. Disillusioned with the empire and India's "satanic" colonial government, in 1920 Gandhi organized the first non-cooperation movement, a campaign of boycotts and protests demanding full independence.

The coming decades would bring a lot more suffering, including Indian service in another world war (which Gandhi opposed this time) and scores of arrests for Gandhi himself.

80

The Choctaw Code Talkers

While the story of the Navajo code talkers of the Second World War is well known, the use of Native American languages as military code actually dates back to the First World War, when the US Army employed members of the Choctaw Nation in Oklahoma to communicate in their native language.

Like many other Native American languages, Choctaw is linguistically complex. Because it was only spoken by a few thousand people in the American West, it was highly unlikely the Germans would have anybody who spoke the language too—or could even identify it.

The US Army employed nineteen Choctaw code talkers toward the end of the First World War, enabling commanders to send urgent verbal messages by wireless or telephone lines tapped by the enemy, without having to bother to encode them first. In order to bring the language up to date for modern military purposes, the code talkers made up new words and phrases to describe things like machine guns (called "little gun shoot fast"). Their quick communication allowed a tricky withdrawal of troops under enemy fire, among other achievements.

The code talkers completely mystified the enemy, as intended. According to one anecdote, a captured German general said he had just one question for his American counterpart: "What nationality was on the phones that night?" The American general replied that of course they were all Americans.

Beginning in the 1980s the Choctaw code talkers were recognized posthumously by the Choctaw Nation, France, and the United States. In 2008 President George W. Bush signed the Code Talkers Recognition Act, awarding Congressional Gold Medals to tribes who provided Native American code talkers.

81

Americans Were Shocked by Racial Equality in Europe

"It is strange to see how the colored troops are received in France," wrote Avery Royce Wolf, a white American volunteering with the French Army, in his diary in September 1917, noting: "There seems to be absolutely no race question, such as exists in America. The negro is accepted everywhere on the same basis as white men. Even the French girls seem to prefer colored soldiers to white soldiers."

American troops used to the regime of racial segregation imposed by Jim Crow laws in the United States were shocked by the formal racial equality prevailing in Europe and especially the "mixing" of genders across racial lines, still an explosive taboo in the American South.

Europe was by no means a post-racial utopia: European colonialism was in full swing, and the imperial projects of Britain and France rested on fundamentally racist assumptions about the supposed superiority of white civilization. Meanwhile many ordinary French peasant folk had never met someone of another race, according to one Senegalese soldier, Sera Ndiaye, who recalled: "Some of the French who had never seen a 'black' man used to pay to come and see us..."

Unlike the United States, with its long history of troubled race relations, France and Britain never enshrined racial segregation in law at home, generally confining formal racial discrimination to their colonial empires. In 1915 France conferred citizenship on the residents of Senegal in return for military service, bringing formal equality to at least one part of its empire, and 160,000 African colonial troops served on the Western Front during the war, where they were billeted with ordinary French families, often forming close relationships (sometimes across gender lines). Another Senegalese soldier, Mbaye Khary Diagne, remembered:

A French girl saw you and felt very pleased by [your appearance]. And she said to you that she wanted to take you to her house to present you to her parents. And you got [an adopted] French family in that way. [But] it wasn't necessary to have love affairs [with them]. From time to time some *marraines de guerre* fell in love with the soldiers they invited home. But generally, they were only friendly relations.

This was the social context that greeted African-American soldiers (and their white comrades) on arrival in France. Unsurprisingly, the absence of Jim Crow–style segregation caused considerable tensions with white soldiers from the American South, who tried to impose their own ways on the French without success, according to Wolf:

The other night there was quite a serious riot between some Americans and the French Colonials who are stationed in this town. These Colonials are colored troops that the French recruit from their foreign provinces. Unlike Americans, the French do not draw a color line, and so these colored troops are accepted by the French girls on the same basis as any other man. This gets under the Americans' skin, so much in fact that there is always trouble whenever the two mix.

In the military sphere African-American soldiers were impressed by the willingness of the Allied supreme commander, Ferdinand Foch, to employ American segregated all-black units in the front lines of the final Allied offensive in the summer and fall of 1918, after the US military had refused to allow them a combat role. Unfortunately, this foreshadowed their return to the US, where the Jim Crow regime and unofficial segregation in northern cities still prevailed.

STDs Were Rampant and Condoms Were Illegal in the US

Sexually transmitted diseases were another bane of Europe's militaries during the First World War, with planners lamenting the millions of duty hours lost, while Christian moralists scolded military and political leaders' lack of care for the souls of their men. None of this made much difference.

During the First World War the British Army treated 400,000 cases of VD, making up one-fifth of all admissions in the BEF in 1916, and Dominions troops were notably afflicted, with an incidence of 110 per thousand among Canadian troops and 130 among Australians. By the summer of 1917, the French Army had recorded 1 million cases of VD since the war began, including more than 200,000 cases of syphilis. On the other side, the German Army generally had lower rates, but in 1915 there were reportedly 30,000 infections with syphilis in the German forces in Belgium alone, and a total of 352,000 cases of syphilis by the end of the war (including relapses).

Most cases of VD were at least somewhat treatable: gonorrhea sufferers could try their luck with an oral remedy involving tropical plant resins, of questionable value and with unpleasant side effects, or go for the more effective "local" solution, with injections of sodium salicylate or toxic metal compounds composed of arsenic or mercury into the urethra. However, there was no guaranteed cure before the introduction of sulfanilamide in 1937. For its part syphilis remained incurable until the mass production of penicillin in 1943.

Military doctors tended to blame STDs on prostitution, with some reason, prompting the French government to officially license brothels with health inspectors. Soldiers home on leave were just as vulnerable: over half the cases of syphilis in the German Army were contracted on the home front. Across Europe, young soldiers were determined to enjoy adult life while they could, and looser sexual mores reflected the growing economic power and sexual liberation of single female factory workers.

Pragmatic as always, the French Army issued condoms to soldiers, but Britain and the US took a much more conservative approach, banning contraceptives, closing brothels, and encouraging abstinence among soldiers, with warnings about the dire consequences for those who strayed.

The very notion of distributing condoms to troops was shocking: Ettie Rout, a New Zealand nurse serving in Egypt, began selling prophylactic kits to troops in 1917, but when she wrote in favor of the idea in the *New Zealand Times*, she was threatened with a £100 fine for undermining morals. Similarly, when the US entered the war, the country's prevailing Christian morality demanded a crackdown on prostitution and continued bans on condom sales, which remained illegal in thirty states.

Rather than hand out condoms, the US Army took a punitive approach, demanding that any man who had sexual intercourse report for medical prophylaxis (flushing the urethra) within three hours of the deed—docking half his pay if he failed to do so. These measures don't seem to have helped much, as the rate of incidence of VD in the US Army actually increased from 103.4 per thousand in 1916 to 113.8 per thousand in 1917; by the end of the war 15 percent of American servicemen had contracted VD, resulting in 7 million lost service days and $50 million in costs.

83

Spanish Flu Actually Started in America, Maybe

Despite being known to history as the "Spanish flu," the influenza epidemic that killed an estimated 50 million people around the world from 1918–1919 may actually have started in the United States of America.

Today flu epidemics usually start in tropical or semitropical Asian, African, or Latin American countries where large numbers of people live in close proximity with farm animals like pigs, ducks, and chickens, giving the viruses a chance to jump from one species to another, a process known as zoonosis.

Doctors and historians studying the 1918 epidemic have proposed origins spanning Southeast Asia, China, India, South Africa, and Mexico, but the most recent research suggests that it may indeed have originated in the United States, where a fair number of people still lived close to farm animals in rural areas. One study suggests that the 1918 flu originated with North American domestic and wild birds, then gradually spread to humans up to twelve years before becoming an epidemic with the first recorded cases at Haskell County and Fort Funston (now Fort Riley), Kansas, in February–March 1918.

The conditions at American First World War training camps like Fort Funston, with large numbers of young people thrown together in cold, poorly insulated barracks and tents, using group latrines, kitchens, and showers, were ideal for spreading respiratory and other diseases—as were the conditions aboard transport ships and in the trenches.

The 1918 flu was especially dangerous due to its virulence and ability to mutate, making it far deadlier in later stages. When the first cases of flu were reported in Haskell County and Fort Funston, Kansas, in February–March 1918, the illness manifested in a fairly mild form but spread quickly, sending 500 enlisted men to the hospital in one week. The flu next showed up among American soldiers in Bordeaux and British soldiers at Étaples, France, in April 1918. At this stage the flu was still relatively benign: although 24,886 soldiers became sick with the flu in May 1918, just seven of these patients died. Around this time it was dubbed the "Spanish flu" because newspapers in neutral Spain, free from wartime censorship, reported the full extent of the epidemic there, creating the impression that Spain was ground zero.

The next phase was far deadlier. In August the supercharged flu appeared almost simultaneously in Brest, France, and Boston, Massachusetts, perhaps having spread back to the US with wounded soldiers. It then proceeded to ravage the war-torn world, passing the trenches with captured troops and crossing borders via neutral countries. By October 1918 the epidemic had spread to twenty-four countries around the world and would ultimately infect an estimated 500 million people, or one third of the planet's population—killing as many as one in ten of the infected—before petering out in late 1919.

Unlike most flu strains, which usually kill children and old people with weak immune systems, the 1918 flu seemed to be especially dangerous for young adults, triggering an overwhelming response from healthy but unexposed immune systems known as a "cytokine storm," essentially causing victims to drown in their own inflammatory secretions. In 1918 the death rate for individuals 15–34 from pneumonia was twenty times the rate in preceding years.

In the United States, by September 1918 epidemics were underway in California and Texas, followed by the Northwest and Great Plains in October. According to the War Department, 26 percent of all US military personnel—over 1 million men—reported sick, and 43,000 died of the flu, including 30,000 in US training camps. Overall the flu killed 675,000 Americans. Largely as a result of the flu, during the First World War more US troops were felled by disease, with 63,114 dead, than in combat, with 53,042 dead.

84

Hitler Was Decorated by a Jewish Officer

The political persona that propelled Adolf Hitler to power was built on his identity as an "ordinary frontline soldier" during the First World War, but it was hugely exaggerated, to say the least.

After joining the Bavarian Army, part of the Imperial German Army, in August 1914, Hitler's List Regiment fought at Ypres with distinction. However, this taste of trench warfare seems to have been enough for Hitler, who snagged himself a relatively safe position as regimental dispatch runner in November 1914, allowing him to spend most of his time at regimental headquarters.

Hitler was a quiet loner, who didn't drink or take part in bawdy sex talk with other dispatch runners at the regimental HQ. Nonetheless in August 1918 Hitler's superior officer, Hugo Gutmann, a Jewish regimental adjutant, nominated him for the Iron Cross First Class in recognition of his services—a standard "political" decoration, scorned by frontline soldiers. Later the Nazi propaganda machine was typically dishonest about the reasons behind the medal: according to one common story, Hitler received the Iron Cross for single-handedly capturing fifteen British soldiers, armed with just a pistol—a fabrication from start to finish.

Gutmann's favor to Hitler hardly won him any gratitude: the dictator's former superior was arrested and imprisoned by the Gestapo in 1937, but veterans of the List Regiment helped him escape to the United States. Gutmann changed his name to Henry G. Grant and lived in San Diego, California, until his death in 1962.

85

"Soldier Millions": Aníbal Milhais

Portugal was forced into the war by the Allies on March 9, 1916, after Britain demanded the Portuguese intern German merchant ships, provoking Germany to declare war in response. Its entry into the war was not insignificant, as Portuguese colonial troops helped chase Lettow-Vorbeck's German guerrilla force across East Africa. However, as a small nation, with a total population of 6 million, Portugal fielded just 55,000 troops on the Western Front, holding around 7.5 miles of front in 1918. The country was also racked by political instability the whole time, including three successful coups, further limiting its ability to contribute. Indeed, it's safe to say Portugal's military record in the First World War was mostly unremarkable—except for one man.

Born in 1895, Aníbal Augusto Milhais was a peasant farmer who was drafted at twenty and sent to the Western Front as part of the Portuguese Expeditionary Force. Soft spoken and modest, he gave no hint of the incredible bravery and physical endurance he would display during the final German offensives in spring 1918.

On April 9, 1918, the Germans unleashed "Operation Georgette," chief strategist Erich Ludendorff's second attempt to break through the Allied lines in Flanders and the Pas de Calais region of northern France, in hopes of defeating Britain and France before American troops began to arrive in large numbers on the Western Front. Like the other spring offensives, Georgette opened with one of the heaviest artillery bombardments of the war, followed by wave after wave of German stormtroopers and infantry, with huge casualties on both sides.

Cracking under the sheer weight of the German assault, tens of thousands of Portuguese and British soldiers retreated pell-mell. Volunteering to stay behind and man a machine gun alone, Milhais continued shooting at advancing German troops for hours, holding off two German regiments singlehanded, only stopping when he ran out of ammunition. After the Germans decided to go around Milhais, cutting him off from his unit, he eluded capture for three days before slipping back across the enemy lines, carrying his heavy Lewis machine gun; along the way he managed to save a wounded Scottish major. Milhais wasn't going to mention his incredible achievements, but the Scottish officer insisted on telling British headquarters, and other witnesses confirmed his report.

Amazingly enough Milhais repeated the feat on July 15, 1918, singlehandedly holding off another German attack with a machine gun, this time allowing retreating Belgian troops to regroup and dig in. Once again, his actions were reported by multiple witnesses.

In recognition of his superhuman accomplishments, the Portuguese government bestowed the country's highest honor, the "Military Order of the Tower and Sword, of Valour, Loyalty, and Merit," on Milhais in front of 15,000 comrades—the only soldier in history to receive the decoration in the field, rather than the palaces of government in Lisbon. He also received the French Legion of Honor. On meeting Milhais, Major Ferreira do Amaral gave him a compliment in Portuguese: "És Milhais, mas vales milhões," roughly translated as, "You're Milhais, but you're worth millions." From then on Milhais was nicknamed Soldado Milhões or "Soldier Millions."

After the war Milhais returned to an economically depressed country and lived in poverty, prompting him to emigrate to Brazil in search of work in 1928. When his hardships were reported by the Brazilian press, a national outcry in Portugal forced the government to grant him a small pension. He died in 1970 at seventy-four in his hometown of Valongo, which had been renamed Valongo de Milhais in his honor.

86

Francis Pegahmagabow, the War's Best Sniper

The deadliest sniper of the First World War was a First Nations Canadian, who was treated as a second-class citizen on returning home.

Born in 1889 on the Parry Island Indian Reserve (later the Shawanaga First Nation reserve) in Ontario, Francis Pegahmagabow was an accomplished sportsman and scout, having learned hunting, fishing, and outdoor survival skills after being orphaned at the age of two. After serving as a marine fire fighter, in 1914 Pegahmagabow volunteered with the Canadian Expeditionary Force despite racial restrictions and first won notice for his marksmanship and scouting ability at the Second Battle of Ypres in April 1915. He earned a reputation for bravery carrying messages during the Battle of the Somme in 1916, and during the Battle of Passchendaele (Third Battle of Ypres) in 1917, now a corporal, he guided reinforcements who had become lost in the trenches to the front, saving his battalion.

> "When I was at Rossport, on Lake Superior, in 1914, some of us landed from our vessel to gather blueberries near an Ojibwa camp. An old Indian recognized me, and gave me a tiny medicine-bag to protect me, saying that I would shortly go into great danger. The bag was of skin, tightly bound with a leather thong. Sometimes it seemed to be as hard as rock, at other times it appeared to contain nothing. At night it seemed to be rising and falling like it could breathe. I kept it with me at all times and I don't think I could have survived the war without it."
> —*Francis Pegahmagabow*

Wounded in his left leg and gassed during the war, "Peggy" claimed over 378 kills, the majority as a sniper, in addition to taking 300 Germans prisoner. Pegahmagabow's commanding officer recommended him for the Distinguished Conduct Medal, but it was never awarded (it's tempting to blame racial discrimination for this slight, but during the war soldiers of all backgrounds expressed scorn for the arbitrary way medals were handed out). However, the Prince of Wales, the future King Edward VIII and Duke of Windsor, personally awarded Pegahmagabow the prestigious Military Medal with two bars, one of thirty-eight Canadians to earn this distinction.

After his discharge in 1919 Pegahmagabow married Eva Nanibush Tronche and eventually fathered eight children, six of whom lived to adulthood. In 1921 he was elected chief of a First Nations tribe, launching him on a political career based on opposition to the Canadian government's discriminatory racial policies, which he condemned as a regime of "white slavery." He opposed the government's attempt to limit official contact with the tribes to white "Indian Agents," who were often corrupt, and asserted First Nations claims to island hunting and fishing grounds in Huron Bay.

Pegahmagabow continued to serve his country, working as a guard at a Canadian munitions plant in the Second World War, and also remained involved in politics: in 1949 he was elected to lead the First Nations national tribal government. He died in 1952 at the age of sixty-one. While his achievements were remarkable, it's worth noting that many of the top Canadian snipers in the war were Inuit or First Nations, reflecting their hunting prowess.

87

Alvin York, Pacifist War Hero

The most celebrated American soldier of the First World War was probably Alvin Cullum York, a pacifist whose wartime feats were later immortalized in the 1941 film *Sergeant York,* in which York was played by Gary Cooper (who won the Academy Award for Best Actor).

York was born in 1887 to a devout Christian family in Tennessee with a total of eleven children, helping raise his younger siblings after his father died. As a young man York joined a Protestant sect called Church of Christ in Christian Union, which had previously split from the Methodist Episcopal Church over its support for the Union in the Civil War. Although not pacifist, the church discouraged violence and participation in politics, and by his own account York held essentially pacifist beliefs. But several petitions he submitted to be categorized as a conscientious objector were denied.

Drafted into the army in 1917, York distinguished himself with his marksmanship and personal bravery. After mentioning his religious qualms, York had a theological debate with his commanding officer, General George Edward Buxton, who apparently managed to convince him that force was sometimes justified in pursuit of justice.

On October 18, 1918, during the final Allied drive to defeat the German Army, York was part of a combat platoon ordered to put a German machine gun nest out of action. Although they succeeded in taking a number of prisoners, enemy fire killed or wounded all the commanding officers, leaving York, a corporal, in charge of the unit.

Determined to complete the mission, York decided to leave his comrades to guard the prisoners and attacked the German machine gun nest himself, killing a number of Germans before running out of ammunition. After emptying his gun but failing to hit York, the German officer commanding the machine gun nest surrendered with his unit. York's platoon returned to their position with 132 prisoners, while York himself is personally credited with killing at least twenty-five Germans and disabling thirty-five machine guns during the attack.

York was first awarded the Distinguished Service Cross, and later the Medal of Honor, for storming an enemy position singlehanded. He also received the French Legion of Honor and Croix de Guerre with Palm, as well as other decorations from Italy and Montenegro.

After the war he returned to Tennessee, where he married his wife Gracie in 1919 and eventually had eight children. Appreciative local businessmen purchased a farm for York, and during the Great Depression he worked as a superintendent for public works projects performed by the Civilian Conservation Corps. He also founded a charity to improve schools in rural Tennessee.

Often sought out by reporters for his take on current events, York never lost his pacifist instincts and later criticized America's decision to fight in the First World War. In the 1930s, with another war looming, he observed: "I can't see that we did any good. There's as much trouble now as there was when we were over there." After suffering a stroke in 1948, his health declined, and he died in 1964 at the age of seventy-six.

The US Navy's Gay Sex Scandal

In an era when homosexuality was not so much a lifestyle option as a crime punishable by long prison sentences and hard labor, it was risky to engage in gay sex acts even in private. Yet plenty of men and women broke the law, moving in a hidden gay subculture and sometimes forming long-term relationships.

Of course, open, if unacknowledged, homosexuality could be useful for blackmail and character assassination: the Austrian arch spy and traitor Alfred Redl was apparently blackmailed by Russian intelligence with threats to expose his gay double life, and in 1916 the British released Irish rebel Roger Casement's letters mentioning homosexual affairs to discredit him after the Irish Rising.

> "I was having such a good time, and even in Holy Ireland I was surprised to meet so many Queens, who took me to tea-rooms and shouted meals for me."
> —*Private Edward Casey*

At the other end of the social spectrum, homosexuals in Europe's big cities relied on anonymity to engage in assignations in places like public bathrooms, parks, nickelodeons, under boardwalks, in back alleys, and near red light districts with female prostitutes. However, they faced periodic police sweeps of the "tearooms," glory holes, and other informal cruising grounds frequented by "queens" servicing "trade," or straight-identifying working-class men.

In the United States as elsewhere, homosexual activity was definitely prohibited by a variety of state laws as well as the federal rules governing the military. Thus public opinion was scandalized by the revelation, in 1919, of a gay sex ring involving US Navy officers and enlisted men and civilians in Newport, Rhode Island, dating back to the war years.

In February 1919, Thomas Brunelle told a fellow patient at the Naval Training Station hospital in Newport, chief machinist's mate Ervin Arnold, about an illicit gay subculture with common haunts at the Army and Navy YMCA and the Newport Art Club, in which straight "trade" from among the navy enlisted men were paid by "fairies" for sex. Arnold investigated personally to verify Brunelle's claims and then, as expected and required, reported the behaviors to his superior officers, including same-sex relations, cross-dressing, and the use of forbidden drugs and alcohol.

The next month the matter came to the attention of Assistant Secretary of the Navy Franklin D. Roosevelt, then age thirty-seven, who as an ambitious young politician was anxious to avoid any appearance of moral laxity. At FDR's instruction Arnold, a former Connecticut police officer, was allowed to organize an independent investigation and did so with remarkable thoroughness, employing over a dozen attractive male agents to infiltrate the Newport gay sex ring (of course this required the investigators to engage in homosexual acts themselves, a small oversight which later proved to be the source of much unwelcome publicity).

In the navy court martial, fifteen sailors were found guilty of sodomy and "scandalous conduct," with two receiving dishonorable discharges while the rest went to naval prison in Maine. However, press coverage of the military tribunal sparked moral condemnation by clergy who expressed disgust at the overzealous methods used in the investigation and also pointed out likely violations of the rights of the accused.

In 1920 FDR accepted the Democratic nomination for vice president and resigned as assistant secretary of the navy. But the Republican sweep in 1920 put the Democrats on the back foot, and in July 1921 a Congressional committee officially rebuked FDR and his former boss, navy secretary Josephus Daniels, over the Newport investigation, lamenting, "Conduct of a character at which seasoned veterans of the service would have shuddered was practically forced upon boys."

However, FDR dismissed the committee's findings as politically motivated, and in August 1921 his political career was interrupted—most at the time thought forever—by an attack of polio while on vacation in Canada.

89

The US Was an "Associated," Not "Allied" Power

In 1914 the "Triple Entente" of Britain, France, and Russia became "the Allies" or the "Entente Powers," fighting the "Central Powers" consisting of Germany, Austria-Hungary, the Ottoman Empire, and Bulgaria. The Allies formalized their military alliance early in the war with the Treaty of London, signed September 5, 1914, and the accession of Italy with a second Treaty of London on April 26, 1915. Japan and Portugal joined the Allies under the terms of separate treaties with Britain.

However, when the United States declared war on Germany on April 6, 1917, it did not join the ranks of the Allied powers. In fact, President Woodrow Wilson insisted on a separate, distinct status for the United States as an "Associated" power, in order to emphasize its freedom from any obligation to respect the European Allies' (potentially sordid) deals and arrangements regarding peace terms, postwar boundaries, and other issues. Prodded by the US, a number of Central and South American nations also signed up for the war as "Associated" powers, generally making symbolic contributions.

Wilson's refusal to recognize Allied claims or become "entangled" in foreign alliances reflected both his idealism and his sense of American exceptionalism, a patriotic belief that the United States is uniquely superior due to its entrenched liberal democracy, based on a perfect, immutable founding document, the Constitution.

Further, like many Americans, Wilson tended to take a dim view of both sides of the First World War: Britain, while admired, was also resented as the former colonial power, and from 1914–1917 the president bitterly criticized the Allied naval blockade on behalf of American commercial interests. Americans also questioned whether the British and French colonial empires could ever be reconciled with democratic ideals.

Unsurprisingly Wilson's insistence on "Associated" status resulted in a lot of friction with the Allied powers. For example, Wilson refused to recognize Italy's claims to predominantly Slavic cultural areas, formerly held by Austria, around the Adriatic Sea—territory promised by Britain and France to get the Italians off the sidelines in 1915. The resulting dispute later fueled Italian grievances about being "cheated" by the Treaty of Versailles, setting the stage for its entry into the Second World War.

Although Wilson supported the creation of a multilateral League of Nations as called for in the Treaty of Versailles, he seemed to view it simply as an American tool for benevolently reordering the world and had no intention of letting other nations wield control over America's actions, as his Republican opponents in the Senate feared. Nonetheless in November 1919 the Senate rejected the Treaty of Versailles over the League of Nations clauses, citing a threat to sovereign US war powers. As a result, the US ended up signing a separate peace treaty with Germany, the Treaty of Berlin, agreed August 25, 1921. Most historians agree America's absence from the League of Nations doomed it to irrelevance.

PART 7

First World War Legacies

IT WOULD BE hard to exaggerate the long-term impact of the First World War, which still shapes the world we live in today. In everything from food and music to sex and literature, the social and cultural changes brought about by the war are everywhere you look.

The most important result of the war was the Treaty of Versailles, which saddled Germany with a gigantic reparations bill while dismembering Austria-Hungary and the Ottoman Empire and establishing a dozen new countries across the map of Europe. Although self-determination for oppressed nationalities was a welcome step forward, many contemporaries believed that the other terms of the Versailles treaty, including a meaningless "war guilt" clause, were unfair to Germany, setting the stage for the Second World War.

The First World War did have some positive results: across Europe and the Americas, women won the right to vote based on their wartime service, representing a revolution in gender relations. However other long-term effects were less visible; for example, for several decades older women were forced to marry younger men because of the male deficit caused by the deaths of 12 million soldiers in the war.

Meanwhile, millions of men who survived the war were left with deep physical and psychological scars: in the first half of the twentieth century most European men of a certain age probably had some degree of post-traumatic stress disorder (PTSD) even if they didn't have "shell shock." The burden of mental illness fell on family members or coworkers in the form of physical violence and other dangerous behaviors. Considering that several generations of European men suffered from long-term mental illness, it's also not hard to see where support for communism, fascism, Nazism, and other violent political movements came from.

The First World War is still with us today, quite literally, in the form of millions of unexploded shells still buried in the soil across Europe, which tragically continue to kill unwitting victims. But some revisionist historians have proposed an even more sweeping theory: the First World War never really ended.

According to this interpretation, the First World War unleashed forces that are still in conflict today, pitting modernity against tradition, technology against faith, and government against the individual. All the conflicts since—including the Russian Civil War, Spanish Civil War, Second World War, Korea, Vietnam, Iran-Iraq War, and now Islamist terrorism—are all just one Great War, which will continue into the indefinite future.

One Good Thing: Women's Suffrage

"If, after this, women in England want the vote, and the men won't give it to them, the men will have a hard time explaining why," the war correspondent Richard Harding Davis predicted in 1916.

Women across Europe and the US demanded the right to vote in recognition of their war service. Before the war even started, women's suffrage had already been granted by a number of state and territorial governments across the United States and British Commonwealth countries.

As predicted, the war turned up the pressure on the male establishment to give women a say. In addition to the simple fact of women's employment sustaining the war effort, some advocates argued that women were more naturally inclined toward pacifism, and would exert a moderating influence on male politicians. A more straightforward argument held that if women didn't get the vote, they might decide not to bear children to replace population lost during the war.

Most men were aware of the debate over women's suffrage, which had made headlines in Britain for over a decade, and a good number of ordinary soldiers and civilians supported women's right to vote, viewing it as the next logical step after enfranchisement of working-class men like themselves. According to Private Edward Roe, a working-class British soldier, a shipboard debate on women's suffrage in 1915 ended in a decisive victory for the side supporting women's rights, with the opponent sent "scuttling down the hatchways."

By the end of the war the barriers were already tumbling across much of Europe and the West. Women played a key role in the Russian Revolution, winning the right to vote in March 1917, and Canada granted women the right to vote in April 1917. On February 8, 1918, King George V gave his assent to the Representation of the People Act passed by Parliament, giving all British women over age thirty the vote—adding 8.4 million new voters at a stroke. The Netherlands and Germany followed in 1919, the latter granting women the right to vote in Article 109 of the new Weimar Constitution. August 20, 1920, brought the ratification of the Nineteenth Amendment to the US Constitution, approved by three-quarters of the states despite outspoken opposition in the South (ultimately Tennessee's legislature voted in favor by a single vote). However, France and Italy, still conservatively Catholic, didn't grant women the right to vote until the aftermath of the Second World War, when most South American nations also granted it. Greece held out until 1952.

Although women in many parts of the world had no hope of winning the right to vote during the First World War due to colonial rule and patriarchal societies, the winds of change were already being felt, with native activists demanding better treatment of women at home, often based on their own personal experiences abroad. Dafadar Ranji Lal, a Muslim Indian serving in the British Army in France, wrote in a letter home to India on November 26, 1916:

When I look at Europe, I bewail the lot of India. In Europe everyone—man and woman, boy and girl—is educated. The men are at the war and the women are doing the work. They write to their husbands and get their answers. You ought to educate your girls as well as your boys and our posterity will be the better for it.

Such sentiments were surprisingly common in letters home written by Indian troops.

Older Women Marry Younger Men

It's no surprise that the First World War had long-lasting effects on European population patterns. In addition to wiping out millions of young men, the war sent birth rates tumbling, as couples delayed marriage and pregnancy due to the uncertainty and disruptions of military service. In Germany the birth rate tumbled by half, from 27 per 1,000 population in 1914 to 13.9 per 1,000 in 1917; in France it fell from 18.2 in 1914 to 9.6 in 1916.

The birth rate would increase again after the war, as society returned to "normal" and people looked to start families. But the war's impact lingered, due to the effective absence of a generation of young men: in 1926, the middle ranks of the French population pyramid slanted heavily female within the age cohort 20–54 (birth years 1871–1905), with 8.5 million men versus 9.8 million women.

This meant that many women were forced to look outside their own age cohort to find male partners, typically with women in their twenties and thirties marrying men in their late teens and early twenties, although the age difference could range into decades (one of the most famous examples is Winston Churchill's mother, Lady Randolph Churchill, who married Montagu Phippen Porch in 1918, when he was forty-four and she was sixty-seven).

It may be no coincidence that this era also saw the rise of the first "heartthrobs," handsome younger men who won the adoration of millions of women around the world, led by Rudolph Valentino, whose 1922 film *The Sheik* sparked the use of the word *sheik* to describe attractive men—or that many "pre-code" Hollywood films depicted strong female characters and sexually aggressive older women.

> "To most young actresses in Hollywood, including me, Rudolph Valentino had about as much sex appeal off the screen as a lemon."
> —*Colleen Moore*

The cross-generational marriages seemed to last: long-term studies showed that women born between 1890 and 1900, reaching prime marriage age during and after the war, were just as likely to be married at age fifty as previous generations. However, the strategy inevitably put them in competition with younger women seeking marriage within their own age group. These, in turn, were also forced to delay marriage as well as marry younger men, leading to a lasting discrepancy in average age of marriage for men and women.

Cities Founded During the War

One good way of reckoning the impact of the First World War is visiting the cities founded during the war, either for war-related purposes or in some other way connected to the conflict.

Murmansk, Russia. When the war cut the Russian Empire off from its normal maritime trade routes via the Baltic and Black Seas, the Allies created a new northern route through the Barents Sea to Russia's Arctic Murman Coast. Here the tsarist regime founded a new port city, Murmansk, connected to the rest of Russia by a new railroad. The town was granted official municipal status in 1916, and from 1918–1920 it hosted British troops aiding White Army forces against the Bolsheviks. During the Second World War Murmansk would play a critical role as one of the main ports for Allied Arctic convoys delivering lend-lease supplies to the Soviet Union. In the Cold War the Murman Coast was an important base for Soviet nuclear submarines. Today it has a population of around 300,000.

Anchorage, Alaska. Anchorage was founded as part of the US military's move to project power in the northern Pacific to counter Japanese expansion in the First World War. After years of delays, in 1914 the US government approved the construction of the new Alaska Railroad, and Anchorage began as a port for the delivery of railroad materials, along with a tent city for around 3,000 workers, originally called "Ship Creek." The settlement attracted more inhabitants and was officially incorporated in November 1920. On March 27, 1964, many of Anchorage's old neighborhoods were destroyed by the massive "Good Friday" earthquake, measuring 9.2 on the Richter scale. Like its Russian twin, today the rebuilt city has a population of around 300,000, making it by far Alaska's biggest city.

Hershey, Cuba. The First World War allowed famed American candy maker Milton Hershey to pursue his dreams of a sugar empire in nearby Cuba. In 1916, concerned about the rising price of sugar due to wartime shortages, Hershey visited Cuba and decided to expand production, calling for a new sugar refinery about 30 miles outside of Havana, along with a whole new town for the workers. The town of Hershey would be a model American community, with suburban homes, a movie theater, baseball diamond, and golf course. After Hershey's death in 1945, his successors sold the town and the rest of the company's Cuban holdings to a Cuban sugar baron; soon after, the refinery and town were nationalized by Fidel Castro, who changed its name to Camilo Cienfuegos in 1961.

Nitro, West Virginia. During the First World War US exports of gunpowder to the Allies reached a peak of 29,377 tons in October 1917—but even this wasn't enough to satisfy British and French demand, along with America's own fast-growing army. To remedy the looming gunpowder shortage, on October 6, 1917, Congress passed the "Deficiency Appropriations Act," which called for the construction of two (originally three) gigantic factories, both able to produce 300 tons of gunpowder per day. The plants were built on the Kanawha River south of Charleston, West Virginia, allowing them to tap abundant hydroelectric power. In just a few months a new factory complex and town, named Nitro for "nitro-cellulose" gunpowder, was built on 1,800 acres of land. By the end of the war it housed some 24,000 people; today it has a population of around 7,000.

93

Chewing Gum

Paul Maze, a French officer serving as a translator in the British Army, recalled his first confusing encounter with their new American allies in 1918: "I remember coming on a battalion for the first time at night, at a time when a barrage was making a fearful din, and I thought they were all talking at once, but on closer inspection it turned out that they were only chewing gum." Maze wasn't alone in noting the American fondness for chewing gum. In 1917 Lord Northcliffe, the British newspaper mogul, observed that the habit was also "rapidly spreading among the English and French."

Chewing gum first became popular in the US beginning in the 1880s, with the introduction of mass-produced *chicle*-based gums. However, the habit didn't cross the Atlantic right away, and before the war Europeans viewed chewing gum with "scorn and derision and treated it as an American habit to be strenuously avoided," according to a trade journal in 1922.

Then during the war Europeans gave the "bovine" practice another look, thanks to its calming effect on the nerves of soldiers under fire and its usefulness quenching pangs of thirst when water was poisoned by the enemy or otherwise unavailable. Chewing gum was also a substitute for cigarettes in frontline trenches, where the light from a single match could draw deadly sniper fire.

Its appeal extended far beyond the trenches. In hospitals and clinics where millions of wounded men were treated, chewing gum was dispensed to help clear the taste of ether after surgery. Perhaps most importantly, American soldiers introduced it to natives everywhere they went: doughboys billeted in French villages and cities won goodwill by handing out large quantities of gum to French children, and later troops from the US Third Army gave chewing gum to German children during the post-war occupation of the Rhine territories. Returning Tommies introduced the practice to civilians across Britain.

Have a Coke

Chewing gum wasn't the only American confection to win over European taste buds during the war: Coca-Cola, the "pause that refreshes," opened its first European bottling plants in Paris and Bordeaux in 1919 (although there were some unfortunate mishaps early on with water quality and dirty bottle caps, leading to cases of vomiting and diarrhea). After this bumpy start, Coca-Cola won widespread popularity in Germany when Ray Powers—an American entrepreneur who first came to Europe as a machine gunner during the war—invented a special refrigerated carrying case, so bar owners could sample their first Coca-Cola ice cold. Powers also hit on the clever idea of marketing Coca-Cola as a hangover remedy.

From 1914 to 1920 chewing gum sales outside the US increased fourteen-fold, and by the early 1920s chewing gum had "become an international product, sold in every country in the world." American companies wasted no time setting up new chewing gum factories to satisfy the fast-growing European market, including in Germany: Wrigley's established its first German production facility in Frankfurt am Main in 1925.

94

Poor Horses: Many Were Eaten after the War

In the plot of the book and movie *War Horse*, the equine title character narrowly escapes being bought and slaughtered by a butcher after the war ends in 1918. This kind of situation was all too common, as hundreds of thousands of horses, having served faithfully during the war, were afterward butchered for meat to feed a starving continent.

Horses and related pack animals provided the backbone of the logistics systems during the war, transporting people, ammunition, and other supplies in all the belligerent nations. In 1914 the French Army requisitioned 740,000 horses, and Britain employed over a million horses, mules, and donkeys over the course of the war, requiring an average shipment of 1,000 horses per week from the US and Canada, and the provision of a total 3 million tons of oats and 2.5 million tons of pressed hay. The US exported a total of 984,000 horses and 342,000 mules from 1914–1918.

Altogether 8 million horses, mules, and donkeys died serving in the war, many of them from starvation, exhaustion, or disease as well as in combat situations, and their bloated corpses were a common sight alongside human dead on all First World War battlefields. From July 1916 to the end of the war in November 1918, the British Army alone recorded 58,090 horses killed and 77,410 wounded by gunfire.

After the war shortages and unrest in Europe, combined with new demands for economic austerity, led to an unsentimental policy of mass slaughter of surplus war horses. Out of 800,000 horses left in British service at the end of the war in 1918, the army kept 25,000 of the youngest, healthiest animals, and sold another 60,000 to British farmers. Lower-quality animals were then auctioned off to European farmers, fetching an average price of £37. Finally, the remainder, consisting of old and sick animals, were sold to knackers who slaughtered them for meat, for an average of £19 per horse. In the end about 61,000 British horses were sold for meat from 1918–1920. In 1919 the US military calculated that the French were eating an average of 2 thousand donkeys and mules and 300 horses per day, and estimated that they had eaten a total 70,000 horses in 1918.

The animals that served in the American Expeditionary Force didn't fare much better. In November 1918, the US War Department estimated that the government owned a total of 477,000 horses, mules, and donkeys. In addition to 182,000 American horses and 29,000 mules sent to France from 1917–1918, the AEF also acquired another 137,000 French horses and 29,000 mules. After losing about 40,000 animals in combat and to other causes, at the end of the war the AEF had 110,000 draft horses and 56,000 mules "surplus." While most of the roughly 350,000 horses and mules lucky enough to remain in the United States were auctioned off to farmers at knockdown rates, 60,000 animals in Europe were slaughtered for meat, with only 200 of the horses originally from the US returning home. This wasn't unusual: out of 136,000 Australian horses sent abroad from 1914–1918, just one, Sandy, returned home.

Paul Kern, the Man Who Never Slept

In addition to around 12 million soldiers and 8 million civilians killed, the First World War left 23 million wounded across Europe, many of them disabled or deformed for life. Men with "shell shock," now recognized as post-traumatic stress disorder, suffered flashbacks and recurrences for decades. Millions more lived uncomplainingly with diseases acquired on foreign service during the war: at least 1.5 million soldiers from all sides contracted malaria in Mediterranean theatres, including 162,000 British and 67,000 French cases in Salonika alone.

There were also a good number of freak injuries and unexplained occurrences, defying medical science. One case that puzzled doctors for decades was that of Paul Kern, a Hungarian junior officer who joined the Habsburg Army as a cadet in 1914 and was shot in the head on the Eastern Front in 1915, the bullet destroying part of his frontal lobe.

After surgery, Kern woke from anesthesia in a military hospital in Lemberg (Lvov)—and supposedly never slept again. Even stranger, according to Ernst Frey, a professor of mental and nervous diseases at the University of Budapest who studied Kern, the ex-soldier said he never felt tired and had no desire to sleep. Sleeping pills had no effect on Kern, and alcohol supposedly made him even more wired.

Doctors predicted that exhaustion would shorten Kern's lifespan, but he lived for another forty years, working for many years as a minor government official without any apparent negative impacts to his work before his death in 1955. During the wee hours Kern said he read, went to cafes, and visited public parks to befriend homeless people, who were always willing to talk.

It's hard to know whether the lack of sleep affected his health; by his own account Kern began taking a one-hour "rest period" in the middle of the night, during which he lay quietly in bed but was fully awake and responsive. Doctors speculate this may have somehow provided enough rest to keep his brain functioning.

The press checked back in periodically with Kern, who was dubbed "the citizen who never sleeps" in Hungary, confirming his continuing insomnia until his death in 1955.

96

Sanitary Napkins Were Invented During the War

During the war large numbers of young women served as nurses, working long shifts in rough conditions, often under enemy fire. In Britain 74,000 women joined Voluntary Aid Detachments, including 38,000 who served in hospitals or as ambulance drivers, while 120,000 Frenchwomen worked as nurses over the course of the war, two-thirds of them unpaid volunteers. In the United States, 21,480 women enlisted as nurses, including 10,000 who served overseas by the end of the war in November 1918.

Military nursing brought large numbers of young and middle-aged women into contact with the latest tools and materials of the medical profession. In 1917–1918 that included bandages made of "Cellucotton," a cheap cotton substitute created by papermaker Kimberly-Clark in 1915 in response to a wartime shortage. Cellucotton's "creped cellulose adding" was manufactured from wood pulp and was five times as absorbent as regular cotton but far less expensive—ideal for cheap, mass-produced bandages.

It wasn't long before nurses and ambulance drivers struggling with their periods on duty discovered that the superabsorbent bandages made effective menstrual pads, easy to change and—best of all—disposable. By 1918 Kimberly-Clark was producing Cellucotton bandages for the US Army and the Red Cross at the Badger-Globe Mill in Neenah, Wisconsin, at a rate of 380 feet per minute (patriotically selling at cost). But executives remained unaware of the novel use nurses had found for the product until after the war, when Kimberly-Clark agreed to buy back the unused stock of Cellucotton from the US government as war surplus, hoping to find some new consumer market.

Then in late 1918 Kimberly-Clark vice president Frank Sensenbrenner learned that young women serving in Europe had been using Cellucotton bandages as sanitary napkins. After two years of study, experimentation, and testing, Kimberly-Clark's designers settled on a rectangular shape with forty plies, or tiny folds, of crepe cellulose, and mass production began in a wood shed near the Badger-Globe Mill. In 1920, over the objections of some scandalized male executives, the company began marketing Kotex sanitary napkins, the company's first consumer brand, to women across the United States.

Advertising was naturally tricky, given the subject matter, but eventually *Ladies' Home Journal*, a top women's magazine with a circulation over 1 million, agreed to run an extremely opaque campaign, kicking off a long tradition of euphemism and allusion in ads for women's health and hygiene products. Many stores refused to carry the product until Kimberly-Clark's marketers hit on a system that allowed women to place their money in a special box, so they wouldn't have to deal with male vendors.

The relative anonymity of mail order changed everything: when Montgomery Ward began offering the product in it its giant catalog in 1926, millions of women started buying Kotex by delivery, and stores soon came round. By 1927 Kotex sales topped $11 million, and during the Great Depression from 1929–1939 sanitary napkins were considered a necessity worth paying for. Along with Kleenex tissues, another Cellu-cotton blockbuster launched in 1924, Kotex helped steer Kimberly-Clark into consumer packaged goods, while inspiring numerous competitors and new products: Tampax, the first tampon, debuted in 1930.

Bringing Yogurt to the World

Yogurt, or milk thickened with bacterial fermentation, dates back as far as 6000 B.C.E., when Central Asian nomads stored milk in cured animal stomachs, releasing enzymes that curdled it, and large quantities were produced in Mesopotamia around 5000 B.C.E. In addition to having a longer shelf life than milk, the ancients recognized its usefulness for calming the digestive system—especially important in an era of primitive hygiene and low culinary standards—as well as cutting the heat of spicy foods and generally being delicious.

The Ottoman Turks brought yogurt to the Balkans beginning in the medieval period—"yogurt" itself is a Turkish word, first recorded in the eleventh century—but for some reason it never crossed over to the rest of Europe until the early twentieth century, when the First World War got things fermenting.

Hundreds of thousands of Europeans (as well as Canadians, Australians, New Zealanders, and Americans) discovered the subtle joy of yogurt during long deployments in the Middle East and Mediterranean. Often forced to eat food that was spoiled or prepared under unsanitary conditions, the Europeans soon came to value yogurt's soothing qualities. One British observer at Gallipoli, Sir Compton Mackenzie, remembered:

> And then somebody who knew what he was talking about said that yorghti was what we should be having every night. Yorghti is sour sheep's milk served in a bowl…and the man who invented it should have as much respect as humanity accorded to Prometheus… Yorghti, whatever way it may be spelled, is a ridiculous name for this life-giving

stuff. At first, in the approved English fashion, the uninitiated members of the mess turned up their noses at it… Presently, however, everybody overcame his insular prejudice…indeed, so successfully that we at the junior end of the table began to look a little anxious as the bowl dallied unduly in the hands of our seniors. There was one older member of the mess whose eyes used to glow like a lover's with real passion when the bowl reached him.

The chaos of war also uprooted Isaac Carasso, a member of a leading Sephardic Jewish family in Salonika, who in 1917 at the age of forty-three emigrated to Barcelona in neutral Spain along with his wife. Carasso noticed that many Spanish children suffered from stomach complaints, and recalled that yogurt was used to treat these sorts of ailments back home in Salonika. After befriending Ilya Ilyich Mechnikov, a Nobel Prize–winning Russian scientist at the Pasteur Institute in Paris who advocated sour milk as a health remedy, Carasso perfected industrial production of yogurt with live cultures of lactic-acid bacilli.

In 1919 he founded a new company called "Danone," named after his fourteen-year-old son Daniel, and opened the world's first commercial yogurt factory. In its early years yogurt was sold as a medicine, available only in pharmacies. After studying business and bacteriology, Daniel succeeded his father at the head of the company in 1939 and went on to build Groupe Danone into a world-straddling food empire, including introducing yogurt to America in the 1940s.

Germany Paid African Soldiers Pensions, If They Could Still Present Arms

The remarkable guerrilla campaign led by General Paul Emil von Lettow-Vorbeck, outwitting and eluding much larger Allied armies across German East Africa (today Tanzania) for four epic years from 1914 to 1918, was only possible because of the bravery, discipline, and endurance of Germany's native African troops, the askaris.

Subject to much stricter discipline and paid more than their counterparts in British and French colonial armies, the askaris were proud warriors who followed Lettow-Vorbeck to the bitter end, only surrendering after the war ended. In fact, on returning home undefeated, Lettow-Vorbeck became the only German general of the First World War to receive a victory parade.

However, after the Weimar Republic paid the askaris their back wages in the 1920s, most Germans forgot that they'd ever had African colonies in the first place. Meanwhile Lettow-Vorbeck, a staunch anti-Nazi, was forced to keep his head down in the 1930s and 1940s, national hero or not.

After the Second World War, Lettow-Vorbeck's former adversary, the South African general and statesman Jan Smuts, found the old general living in poverty in Germany and arranged for a small pension to be paid to him. Then in 1959, at the age of eighty-nine, Lettow-Vorbeck went back to Tanganyika (as it was called until 1964) where he was warmly received by his former troops, but troubled to see many destitute.

Lettow-Vorbeck spent the remaining five years of his life lobbying the West German government to recognize the askaris' service for Germany in the First World War and compensate them with a pension. Prompted by the attention around Lettow-Vorbeck's death in 1964, West Germany finally agreed to pay a stipend to any surviving askaris.

However, this was more complicated than it sounds: many of the former native soldiers had no formal birth certificates or identification papers, and most of the records had been lost or destroyed anyway, so there was no way to confirm that they actually served. Some still had rifles, bayonets, uniforms, or old pay books as keepsakes after five decades, but scam artists could easily obtain these to pass themselves off as veterans.

The West German banker dispatched to Dar es Salaam to pay out the askaris' stipends half a century after their service hit on a simple solution. There was one thing every veteran of the super-disciplined German Army was guaranteed to be able to do: present arms and march. Amazingly, fifty years later every single one of the askaris could perform the thirty-two-step Prussian drill march flawlessly, with a broomstick in place of a rifle.

99

People Are Still Being Killed by Old Munitions

During the First World War the opposing sides fired around 1.5 billion shells, along with 50 billion rounds of small arms ammunition. However, hundreds of millions of shells didn't detonate, with an overall failure rate of around 15–30 percent during the war, leaving battlefields strewn with unexploded munitions, some of which are still killing people a century later.

The magnitude of the problem matched the scale of the conflict. Immediately after the war, French authorities cordoned off around 65,000 square kilometers in the country's northeast in order to allow military, police, and civilian contractors to dispose of most visible leftover munitions. However, there was no way they could possibly find and remove all the shells, even with the introduction of portable metal detectors in 1947.

In order to minimize the danger, certain areas remained off limits for even longer after the war: the "Red Zone," concentrated around the Western Front, consisted of around 1,200 square kilometers of French territory closed to ordinary activities including housing, farming, and forestry, allowing the areas to return to nature as much as possible (in many areas the soil is also poisoned by lead, mercury, or arsenic from used shells).

Over the years most of the Red Zone was returned to habitability, but a considerable amount of land remains closed to the public for safety reasons: by one estimate around 168 square kilometers—an area about the size of Paris—are still off-limits across northern France. There are still over 10 million unexploded shells under the soil at Verdun alone, prompting tourist authorities to restrict access to certain areas, while a ten-person specialist team continues to lead shell removal efforts.

Indeed, the job of cleaning up the shells in reclaimed areas is by no means finished, and the inhabitants of reclaimed land are constantly uncovering old artillery shells in the soil, most from the First World War. Every year the "Iron Harvest" by French and Belgian farmers unearths about 900 tons of old munitions, and from 2010–2014 the Belgian military said it cleared 629 tons of old munitions.

> "I can't tell you how many I find sometimes. Even in the forest…
> When we go mushroom-picking, I see a hundred shells."
> —*Roland Dabit, Verdun resident*

Most of the shells remain duds, but tragically leftover explosives have killed a number of unlucky individuals since the war ended. At Ypres, Belgium, alone, 358 people have been killed and 535 injured by exploding First World War munitions over the years. In March 2014, as the centenary of the war loomed, two construction workers were killed in Ypres when a derelict shell exploded under the warehouse where they were working. Of course, clearing bombs is always dangerous work: in 2007 two specialists from Metz died when the shell they were moving exploded, and another bomb disposal expert died in Arras in 1998 while trying to defuse a shell.

Germany Paid Off Its Last Reparation in 2010

After four years of all-out war, the victorious Allies forced Germany to officially accept "blame" for the war in the Treaty of Versailles, then saddled the Germans with a massive reparations bill, supposedly in compensation for all the damage and destruction. Unable to persuade the United States to forgive their war debts, the British and French hoped to use German reparations payments to finance the repayment of their own debts to American banks and the Treasury.

Because the sums involved were so huge—in 1921 Germany owed 132 billion gold marks or $33 billion to the Allies, or around $402 billion today—payments were scheduled over a very long time. Despite some interruptions and unwise moves (in the 1920s Germany induced hyper-inflation by printing cash) the financial system has been steadily processing the loan and reparations payments, year in, year out, long after most people who experienced the war are dead.

On October 3, 2010, the German government made the last reparation payment from the First World War, redeeming bonds that were issued from 1924–1930 to cover a refinancing of the reparations system under the Dawes Plan, named for American banker Charles Dawes. Hitler refused to make any more reparations payments in 1933, and the bonds became worthless, at least temporarily: after the Nazi defeat, in 1953 West Germany agreed to honor some of the country's prewar financial obligations. Following reunification Germany stepped up the repayments in 1995.

The Allies have been slowly repaying their war debts as well. On March 9, 2015, the British government announced that it had repaid the outstanding £1.9 billion of debt from the First World War, redeeming war bonds carrying a 3.5 percent interest rate and held by around 120,000 investors.

The German Ship That Inspired *The African Queen* Is Still in Service

Most passengers at the quay at Kigoma, Tanzania, waiting for the ferry amid fruit sellers and goods awaiting transport on Lake Tanganyika, probably don't know that they are about to board a piece of living history. The MV *Liemba*, a 234-foot ferry boat operated by the Marine Services Company Limited of Tanzania, began her life as a very different ship over 100 years ago—the First World War German gunboat *Graf von Goetzen*.

Simply getting the *Graf von Goetzen* to Lake Tanganyika required a feat of engineering. After being built in Germany in 1913, the ship was disassembled, packed in 5,000 crates, and shipped to Dar es Salaam in German East Africa. Then the crates were transported hundreds of miles inland by rail, crossing mountain ranges to reach Kigoma, where the *Graf* was finally assembled by hundreds of native laborers on the shores of Lake Tanganyika.

> "It is both the duty and the tradition of the Royal Navy to engage the enemy wherever there is water to float a ship."
> —*Admiralty directive*

At the beginning of the war the *Graf von Goetzen* dominated Lake Tanganyika along with two smaller gunboats, the *Kingani* and *Hedwig*, denying this important 418-mile-long transportation link to enemy troops coming from the neighboring Belgian Congo or British Zambia.

But the Royal Navy Admiralty was not to be put off. The British disassembled two 40-foot-long motor launches, the *Mimi* and *Toutou*, and shipped them by sea to Capetown, then overland 3,000 miles—some places by rail, others with oxen and two steam tractors along with hundreds of human carriers—north to the Belgian Congo.

After reassembling the boats, the *Mimi* and *Toutou* were launched on Lake Tanganyika at Lukuga just before Christmas 1915. On December 26, 1915, expedition commander Geoffrey Spicer-Simson had a stroke of good luck, catching the small German gunboat *Kingani* out of range of the *Graf von Goetzen*'s protective fire. The prize, renamed *Fifi*, made a substantial addition to the strength of the small British fleet. Then in January the British boats trapped *Hedwig* on a scouting expedition and sank the boat after a direct hit to the boiler.

Lake Tanganyika remained under the domination of the *Graf von Goetzen*'s heavy guns until mid-1916, when the Allies advanced into German East Africa from all sides, threatening to deny the ship a base for fuel, resupply, and refitting. The guns were removed to provide desperately needed artillery for the small German and native guerrilla army led by Paul Emil von Lettow-Vorbeck, and on July 26, 1916, the German commander scuttled the ship to deny its use to the enemy, taking care to cause as little damage as possible so it could be resurrected after the war (considerably less dramatic than the cinematic fate of the *Königin Luise*, the fictional ship in *The African Queen* inspired by the *Graf von Goetzen*).

The *Graf von Goetzen* was first raised by the Belgians in 1920 but sank again during a storm. It then remained a submerged hulk until 1924, when the British salvaged the ship largely intact. After a three-year refitting the ship entered commercial service as the MV *Liemba*, and has continued ferry service with few interruptions to the present day. Today the *Liemba* is still favored by small-time merchants and vendors as a fast, cheap way of making the rounds on Lake Tanganyika, stopping at twenty-one ports of call on a typical five-day round trip.

INDEX

Index